FINDING
YOUR
SWEET SPOT

Letting Go of the Familiar for Your Calling

By
LESLIE V

This book is dedicated to God-Father, Son,
and Holy Spirit, and to
my mom and dad.

ACKNOWLEDGMENTS

I would like to acknowledge some people and organizations that played a role in the inspiration of this book. To my cousin Leah (Maria), who was with me for a good portion of this journey.

To my writing instructor, Dawn Montefussco, for all her encouragement during the writing process.

To Pastor Stroud, who knew there was a book in me.

To my sisters in the Lord, who gave lots of encouragement.

To HCL 22 for training me and helping me to complete what I started.

FOREWORD

"Be yourself, the world worships the original."

— Ingrid Bergman

The world has experienced more shared trauma in these last few years than in all of human history. I say this not to downplay trauma in the past, but because before the internet we were not as aware of each other's pain, or love, to the degree that we are now. This is both a blessing and a curse, depending on how you look at it. That's why it's so important for us to share our stories in empowering ways, and to trust God and ask for guidance.

When Leslie asked me to write the foreword for this book, I was truly in a dark space of disillusion. I had been praying daily for a sign and I realized I needed to go deeper inside myself and wait for God's voice.

Suddenly, it hit me that I was past my deadline and so I immediately printed out *Finding Your Sweet Spot* and began reading.

Her words pierced my heart and broke it open. I was especially moved by the following: "God made you for so much more. If there is a longing inside you for something more or better, that's God working in you. If there is an inner battle within, that is God trying to lead and guide you into truth. The Holy Spirit may be speaking to you, saying, 'It's time. It's time.'" Reading this, I cried tears of joy, knowing I had received the answer I'd been seeking.

I have been successful at many things in my life and I have stretched out of my comfort zone many times, but it's during the darkest times that I get stuck and fear there is no way out. What I learned from Leslie is this: God wants us to be happy and wants us to follow our calling, which is His calling for us. In doing this, we also find peace in His guidance.

My Goliath was my inner world of depression and anxiety because of the pandemic. I had become frightened of the boogie man. There was nothing to fear, and yet I felt captive in my own mind. When I read Leslie's book, a wave of peace came over me. I heard a voice that told me to look around and see my blessings. When you come from a place of gratitude, you will always find God's help. I saw my home and my dog and the love of my friends and family. I just needed to look up.

Again, Leslie's book was the sign I had been waiting for and was exactly what I needed at the exact right time. Then I remembered: Trust God. I needed to trust Him more than ever before and to let every sign lead me back to a place of deep inner peace. With inner peace, you are unstoppable.

Leslie has a beautiful knack for storytelling, and she has a deep faith in the Lord that penetrates every page. If you are needing a new boost of confidence to follow a dream, or you need a jump-start to get you back on track, *Finding Your Sweet Spot* is the book to read.

There are no limits to what we can achieve when we surround ourselves with people who lift us up and remind us that we always can do what seems impossible at first.

Keep this book close to you and share it. Leslie's words are made to be part of many people's lives. It's in giving that we learn to receive.

With Love and Gratitude,

Dawn

dawnmontefusco.com
https://www.facebook.com/DawnMontefusco/
oneshortbook.com
~~~~~~~~~~~~~

TABLE OF CONTENTS

PART 1

EXPOSED AND STUCK

THE INTRODUCTION

I was born and raised in Carrollton, Georgia, a small town about forty-five minutes from Atlanta. Growing up, church was a huge part of my life. Every Sunday, I went with my mom, and I loved it because it was filled with her sisters, my cousins, and longtime friends.

At church, everything was familiar. There was a devotional service with congregational songs and three prayers. We even knew who would do the last prayer. As kids, we sat in the back and said the familiar part of the prayers with the deacon while he prayed.

After the devotional service was over, it was time for the choir. The first song was usually a fast one to get everybody up on their feet and moving. Their last song, before coming out of the choir stand, was slow and moving. It was setting the atmosphere for the preaching that was to follow.

Then everybody would stand as the pastor read the scripture that would go with his sermon for the week. When he got to the middle of the sermon, his voice would change. In the Baptist Church, we called it "whoop." This got the crowd up and they would shout back at him in response to what he was saying.

Afterward, we would get together and talk. It was a time of fun and laughter, with the adults catching each other up about the past week and I and the other teens entertaining ourselves with the goings-on we'd observed during the service.

"Did you see," one girl asked, "how that usher almost got hit in the face when that woman lifted her hands and started shouting?"

When the Spirit moved on someone, an usher would always come by with a fan and wave it to calm them. The usher had to be careful, though, or they would get hit. They never knew when a person's arms would go up in response to what was being preached. We would say that he or she "got happy" during the church service. That particular woman was so moved by the Spirit she nearly lost her hat three times!

For the longest time, that was our Sunday routine: the service, the chit-chat, the laughter, then we'd leave and do it all over again the following week. And I was happy with that. It was …well…easy like Sunday morning.

Then something happened. God exposed me to something different.

When we're exposed to something different, one of two things happens. Either we don't like this new thing – in which case life goes back to business as usual – or we do like it and realize we have a decision to make. Do we stay the same, or follow this new path presented to us?

This book is for those who know God has more for them than what they are currently experiencing. As you come on my journey with me, you will also be going on your own journey. There will be questions along the way to help you see where you are on this journey and how to move forward.

What do you want? Do you want to stay stuck in the same place, or do you want to move forward? What can you do to find *your* sweet spot?

CHAPTER

To Something Different

There I was, enjoying life and enjoying church. I was minding my business, doing the same old thing. Each Sunday I got up early in the morning and turned on the radio to listen to gospel music. Then I turned on the television to watch the gospel show, which featured well-known gospel singers of the day. The host even interviewed the artist so we could see what they were up to. Sunday was the only day of the week these shows were on and Mom and I looked forward to them each week.

All the while, we'd be getting ready for church. We had to be cute for the service. The hair had to be done whether in a pony-tail, straight or even up into a ball. There were no torn stockings. The high heels got a fresh polish. Before we left, we'd take one last glance in the full-length mirror to make sure everything was in place. Yes, we were looking good. Then we'd get in the car and drive fifteen minutes down a curvy back road and make it in plenty of time for the eleven-a.m. service.

One morning, Mom and I were going through our regular routine. We knew exactly how we would spend the next few hours: the devotional service; the singing choir; the preaching of the preacher; the people "getting happy."

That's when something different happened. I turned the TV to a Christian program. The preacher didn't whoop, but he taught the Word of God in a way I had never heard before. And I liked it.

He talked about things not working out as Paul and Silas had hoped. They were doing God's work. They were preaching God's Word. Yet they found themselves beaten and put into prison.

Although the situation was bad, they didn't get offended by God. Instead, at midnight they sang praises to Him. Because of their praise, everyone's chains loosened and the prison doors opened. None of the prisoners tried to escape. As a result, salvation came to the person in charge of the prison and his entire household.

The message to me was that things will go wrong in life. I had the choice to be offended at God or have faith in Him. As I had faith in Him, wonderful things could happen even when they seemed impossible.

As I watched the show, something clicked into place. Preaching wasn't so the congregation could get a high feeling from the "whoop." It was for each person to receive the Word of God and apply it to the issues in their life. Wow, what a revelation. That was not only what I wanted; it was what I needed.

There was a particular couple on the show who inspired me. They were regular, average, everyday people, yet they had a connection and confidence when it came to God that I had never seen before.

The man talked about how he used to sing in bars and had no desire to have anything to do with God. His wife, Gloria, talked about how she'd never wanted to marry a preacher.

They were living in desperate times, in a small house with no furniture and a small income. One day Gloria took out the Bible her mother-in-law had given them. On the first page, her mother-in-law had written "Matthew 6:33." Gloria went to the scripture, which read, "Seek first the kingdom of God and His righteousness and all these things will be added onto you." She then said out loud, "God, here I am, if you can do anything with this life, I give it to You."

She began seeking God, reading the Bible, and praying. And as she got to know God, things were added to her and her household, things like furniture to her home and a better income.

Since they were everyday, ordinary people and God helped them, I thought to myself, *Maybe God will help me too.* Since He cared about the sparrow and took care of them, maybe He would take care of me. This teaching gave me hope. God was real. He cared about my actual situation. It was another huge revelation for me.

Many of us have been a part of churches like mine. We knew how the service would flow from beginning to end. We repeated the process again and again. Many times we were happy and content. We never exposed ourselves to anything different.

As I mentioned earlier, when we're exposed to something different we find ourselves faced with a decision. We are at the fork in the road. Have you ever been in this situation? Have you ever exposed yourself to something new and liked it? What happened?

In my case, liking this different church, this different way of preaching, caused conflict to rise inside of me. I knew the old wasn't enough, yet I tried to make it work because for so many years it *had* worked, and I was loyal to it. Yet, what I heard on TV was calling me to change my thinking.

This can't just be on TV, I thought. *Surely somebody teaches like this in my area.*

I knew I had to be like Peter, who followed Jesus out of the boat and stepped onto the water. I had to find this place. I was sure it was out there. I couldn't settle for less. I had to find the sweet spot.

CHAPTER

To Wanting and Needing Something New

Oh, what a predicament I was in! Should I stay at my church? Or should I go? I couldn't help but think about the Word taught differently. I still enjoyed the choir, but when the whoop began it was time to close the Bible and watch. I couldn't take any notes then. All I could do was watch the preacher. My spirit wasn't being fed.

Why couldn't things just stay the same? Like many of us, I like predictable things; I like A-B-C and 1-2-3. I like the steady, the consistent, the familiar. I like to know how things are, and what's coming next. That's what my Sunday routine was for me. Everything worked like clockwork, like A-B-C.

I recalled that old gospel song, "Old Time Religion." The chorus went, "Give me that old-time religion. Give me that old-time religion. Give me that old-time religion. Lord, it's good enough for me!" According to the song, old-time religion had been good enough for Peter and Silas, and for "our mothers," so it should be enough for me, right? Except it just wasn't. It was familiar and comfortable, yes, just the way I liked things. But now, after hearing the Word of God, the familiar was no longer satisfying. I was hungry for something more.

I then had a sense of a song by the group Commissioned, which said just the opposite. It was about moving away from the ordinary to seek out the kind of pure love that calls to our hearts. The point of the song is that we need to look no further than Jesus.

At this time, I still hadn't quite put together what my hunger pains were. I hadn't yet put my finger on the deep longing in my heart that could not be quenched with "Old Time Religion." However, I knew I had to go for the new – the unfamiliar. I not only wanted it; I needed it.

2 Corinthians 5:17 told me, "I am a new creature in Christ." As a new creation, I needed something new. I had a revelation on being made new to do new things. I discovered I was not to be stuck in the old ways of doing things. Behold, God is doing a new thing. Since God was doing something new, I wanted to see what He was up to.

All along, God worked in me to do according to His good pleasure. All along, God stirred and moved through the Holy Spirit inside me. He led and guided me into the truth I could understand.

In the past, we've all been through something like this. We experienced an inner struggle because part of us wanted the same familiar things, while another part wanted an adventure. It wanted God's will. Yet we often stay stuck in the familiar and never reach the ideal.

God made you for so much more. If there is a longing inside you for something more or something better, that's God working in you. If there is an inner battle within, that is God trying to lead and guide you into the truth. The Holy Spirit may be speaking to you, saying, "It's time. It's time."

What are you going to do about it? Are you willing to stay stuck another twelve months, fifty-two weeks, three hundred and sixty-five days? Or are you ready to live your best life ever, starting now? What is one way you can get moving?

CHAPTER

To Stepping Out of the Comfort Zone

What is the comfort zone? A comfort zone is a place that feels familiar to a person. In that place, the person is at peace and has less anxiety and stress. It's a beautiful place, but nothing grows there.

The church I grew up in was my safe place. It was filled with my family and friends, with people who had watched me grow up. There were people I had grown up with and those I had watched grow.

There was an evangelist that I trusted, so one Sunday after church I sought out her advice.

After telling her my story, I asked, "Do you know of any churches I could visit?"

"Maybe you want to try this church on Columbia Drive," she replied. "If you go there, it's possible you may not want to go anywhere else."

Hearing her words put a big grin on my face and peace in my heart. I thanked her, then I went to talk to my cousin. I told her what the evangelist had told me about this new church and asked her if she wanted to go with me.

"Yes, let's do this," she said, "When do you want to go?"

This was the beginning of me stepping out of my comfort zone. I was still a member of my church – still had one foot in the safe place – but I was willing to see if I could find what I was looking for.

Oftentimes we stay in our comfort zone because it feels safe. So safe, in fact, that we don't stop to think that it might actually be dangerous. We get complacent.

The world is constantly changing around you, and if you don't change with it you are not going to grow. What one small step can you take now to move outside your comfort zone? If you're unhappy with your family, plan a fun event. If you are unhappy with your job, look at your skills and redo your resume. If you need help, get advice from someone you trust, as I did with the evangelist.

That first small step out of my comfort zone turned out to be an amazing experience. I loved everything about it – the praise service, and harmony of the choir, with the sopranos, altos, and tenors all blending beautifully together. They sang songs that were fast and upbeat, songs I knew from the radio. They sang songs I'd grown up with from my church, and they sang slow songs that were unfamiliar.

The praise team also got me excited. Until then, I had only been to devotional service, which was quite different.

Now the Word of God was coming through, and it was outstanding. The pastor even explained the song selections.

"We purposely put the unfamiliar songs in the praise service," he said, "We want a diverse church. So we chose different music."

But it was his next words that really struck me: "If you want the congregation to look like you, sing songs by those artists. If you want the congregation to include people who don't look like you, sing different songs."

I got this revelation on praise and worship all because I had stepped out of my comfort zone. It had exposed me to something I needed and wanted. I became a regular visitor at this church and was soon presented with another opportunity.

Knowing I worked with music, the pastor said, "We're starting a choir with our youth. Would you be interested in working with them?"

I told him I would. It was my first reward for stepping out of my comfort zone and into my sweet spot. You too will be rewarded when you move away from the familiar and toward something new. You may also be reminded of rewards you have missed while clinging to the safety of your comfort zone, but don't get too bogged down by that. Just work with where you are now.

As I mentioned, this was just my first step in the journey. I would continue to take many small steps, and I still am today. Do you think writing a book is comfortable? It's not, but here I am.

Remember, the comfort zone can also be a danger zone. Your fears are often what keep you stuck there. To escape you have to move toward those fears like David did.

David moved toward Goliath with a slingshot and rock. He wasn't like the Israelite army, who cowered in fear as Goliath taunted them. They saw how big he was. Since they saw themselves smaller, they hid. They ran the opposite way. They were in the comfort zone. Instead, David ran toward Goliath – the thing feared by most – and was able to do the "impossible." He slew Goliath. He won.

God is not a respecter of persons (Acts 10:34). If David won, so can you. Will you face your fear? Are you ready to do the uncomfortable things until you feel comfortable? I'm sure David didn't hit the target when he first started using his slingshot, but eventually he killed the lion, the bear, and the giant. You can do the same.

When was the last time you stepped out and did something you didn't feel comfortable doing? What is one thing you can do today to defeat your "Goliath" and move out of your comfort zone?

CHAPTER

To Unexpected Turns

According to Revelation 13:7-8, God opens doors no man can shut. He closes doors no man can open. When I was at my old church, I worked with the youth and the choirs. Most of my Sundays were full of responsibilities, leaving me little opportunity to even think about other churches, let alone visit them.

Then God opened the door. One day, some new people came into the church and wanted to start a choir. One of the choirs I worked with sang two Sundays. The pastor gave them one of those Sundays, which freed up time for me. I decided to use that time to visit other churches.

Remember, God is not a respecter of persons Acts 10:34; He doesn't open a door for one and not another. We've all had doors open for us, yet we didn't always walk through those doors. We didn't take the chance. Sometimes, we didn't even see the open door; we just talked about how that wasn't right or this wasn't fair.

Someone may have looked at my situation differently, they may have seen it as the pastor taking something from me. Instead, I chose to see it as an open door, as a chance to try something new. It wasn't a big step, but it was a step, and I took it. Will you?

The more time I spent in the new church, the more I fell in love with praise service. I also realized that I had never really liked devotional service, it was just all I knew.

I even attended their Bible study. In taking that step of faith, I saw the importance of praise and worship. Also, I enjoyed the teaching of the Word.

In the meantime, I was still working with the youth at my original church. I invited them to a Sunday night service at the church I was visiting, and they liked it so much that they came a few more times.

Then one Sunday night our leader from the youth ministry asked the youth, "Since we are in charge of service on the second and fifth Sundays, couldn't we have praise and worship service instead of a devotional service?"

Now, if you know anything about young people, you know their responses are often things like,

" I don't know"; "I don't care"; or "I guess so."

They also usually wait to see how their peers react and follow suit. This time they didn't do or say any of that. Instead, they all immediately said, "Yes!"

Hearing this, I was both surprised and excited. I was also nervous. I had never done anything like this before. I had just learned about praise and worship myself. But since they were so enthused about it, I couldn't back out.

I watched the praise team at the new church closely. I listened to find solid praise and worship songs. I learned those songs, then taught them to the youth in three-part harmony. Once the groundwork was done, it was time to debut praise and worship at my church.

How did it go? Was it a hit? Was it successful? Well, there were mixed reviews.

The deacons were angry because we only had one prayer instead of the three prayers in traditional devotional service.

"They are trying to take prayer out of the church," one of them said.

On the other hand, the youth loved it, and so did I. So we continued despite the naysayers.

Sometimes doors open for us, but we do nothing. We make excuses about why we can't do it. We keep telling ourselves the same old stories, and these stories keep us from walking through doors that God opened for us.

Walking through these doors takes you closer to finding the sweet spot.

For me, taking a step of faith brought an unexpected turn. It opened up a door to do our own praise and worship. However, we would need to take many more steps of faith to get the project off the ground. Obstacles came up; the naysayers kept talking, but we kept going. Now, though I have been gone for many years, I know they are still having praise and worship at my old church.

I still sometimes fear walking through the doors of opportunity. But I know that if I let fears stop me, I will be stuck forever. Remember, FEAR stands for false evidence appearing real, so even though we don't know what's on the other side of that door, it's time to take a chance.

Yes, unexpected turns happen in life. They often seem to come out of the blue, but God works things out for the good of them that love Him and are called according to His purpose (Romans 8:28).

God has a plan and purpose for you. When obstacles arise (John 16:33) – and they will – will you quit or press forward? What can you do to find your sweet spot?

Are you ready to take a step of faith through the open door? Are you tired of discussing what's unfair? Are you ready for more? What's one thing you can do? What open- door opportunity is there for you right now? Where can you walk out in faith?

Walking through an open door may require changes. Are you ready to learn something new in order to go through the door? Are you willing to research and figure things out? Will you keep going, despite the naysayers?

Although I was happy with the recent changes with the praise team, it wasn't enough. The service at my church would remain the same devotional service it had always been, and now that I had been exposed to the teaching of the Word and praise service, it wasn't enough. The choice became obvious: it was time to go somewhere else.

Still, I was conflicted. What about the church I had attended all my life? What about my family and friends? What about the position I had and the impact on the youth? How could I leave? Why should I *have* to leave? It would never be enough, but I had to keep holding on. Things had to get better, right?

Look at this free resource. www.findyoursweetspotseries.com/resources

CHAPTER

David and Goliath

I went to the new church ready to receive the Word. I left mad. Why was I mad? It was because of David and Goliath. All my life I had heard the story of David and Goliath – how David had defeated Goliath with a slingshot and a stone. How David picked five smooth stones just in case he missed. That's what I'd gotten all my life at the church I grew up in, so when we turned the Bible to 1 Samuel 17, that's what I was expecting to hear. However, that's not what I got.

As I listened to the preacher break it down line by line, I was amazed by how much more there was to the story, and mad that nobody had ever told me before. In hindsight, I believe they didn't know it either. They were just preaching what they had heard. It got passed down over and over. I believed this, and yet I still felt cheated.

This time, the pastor started with verse one. Verses one through three painted the picture of two opposing armies facing each other, ready for battle. Let's say the good guys are our guys, our team, our family, and our friends. The bad guys are our enemies known as the Philistines.

The Philistines sent out Goliath, who was over nine feet tall and carried a bronze sword. His armor weighed about one hundred and twenty-six pounds; the tip of his spear was over fifteen pounds alone! Like most difficult situations in our lives, Goliath looked scary.

It was even scarier when he spoke. Basically Goliath said, "Why are you here? I am the head of this army. Let's get this over with. Send a man to me and let us fight. If he kills me, we will be your servants. If I kill him, you will be our servants. I defy the armies of Israel this day. Send somebody to me. Let's do this."

When Saul, the king, and the Israelites army heard those words, they were afraid.

As we dropped to verses 20-23, Goliath came out as always. The Israelites saw him, heard his words, and were afraid. David, however, had a different perspective. Instead of running away, he started gathering information on the reward for the person who defeated Goliath.

David said, "Who is this uncircumcised Philistine that he should defy the armies of the living God?"

David knew he had a covenant with God; he also knew that Goliath did not have such a covenant. David would stand up for God, and he knew God wouldn't let him down.

David asked other questions as well, so many that he got the attention of Saul, the king of the Israelites.

Saul told David, "You are not able to do this."

Isn't that like the devil, always telling you what you cannot do?

After Saul told David what he could not do, David recited his past victories. He had killed the lion and the bear, and since God helped him do that, he knew God would deliver him from the hand of Goliath. David used his past victories, looked at his present circumstances, and trusted God.

In verses 38-39, Saul allowed David to go. Saul dressed David up in his armor, but David couldn't use it. He couldn't walk in the armor. He hadn't tried or tested it. So he took it off and grabbed what he knew.

He then picked out five smooth stones – the extras in case Goliath's brothers showed up – and put them in his bag. He took his staff and slingshot.

It was about to be on. As big as Goliath was, he had an armor bearer that went before him. When he saw David, Goliath began to taunt him. He was also telling David what he could not do.

In verse 48, David ran toward Goliath. He put his hand in his bag, took out a stone, slung it, and struck the Philistine in the forehead. That stone sank deep into his forehead and Goliath fell. Then David took Goliath's sword and cut off his head. David won.

Let's break this story down even further. You're on one side of the battle line. On the other side are your troubles. Suddenly your biggest enemy, your biggest fear, and your biggest mindset issues stand up and start talking. You feel like a nine-foot giant is attacking you with words.

If we continue to listen to Goliath, things get scary. We begin to act as the Israelites did. Somehow we must gain a unique perspective, as David did. Instead of being defeated in life, David looked for the reward for winning the battle. David believed in God. David believed there was something higher than himself. David stood up for God and knew God would help him. Do you?

Why not ask positive questions? What if I win, what will I get? Will I find the sweet spot? When I defeat this current giant, how will my life look differently?

Saul told David, "You can't do this." These words are like the limiting beliefs that rise within you, saying you're too old, too young, the wrong gender, the wrong race, too little, too big, not good enough, inexperienced, et cetera.

What victories can you recite to the "Sauls" in your life? What will you say to those limiting beliefs in your mind? How has God helped you in the past? Will you use those victories to win now? Like David, you can win.

CHAPTER

Six

To Another Church?

While I was visiting this church, another unexpected turn occurred. My cousin got another job with a new supervisor. One Saturday, we were headed out to a movie when she said, "My supervisor gave me a CD of her pastor." She grinned big. "After the movie, we've got to go to my house and listen to it."

Since she was excited about it, I was too. When we got to her house, she took out some paper and pens so we could take notes, then turned on the CD, and we took notes.

Oh my God, what a message that Pastor brought forth! I don't remember everything he said, but I do remember how moved I was.

I remember looking at my cousin several times and saying, "You've got to play that part again."

A one-hour message took us about ninety minutes to get through. Although I had never heard a message like this, it struck in my spirit-my inner being. I just knew this was the truth. It was great! It was awesome! We had to visit this church. My cousin agreed.

We went on my next Sunday off, and oh my God, it was awesome, wonderful, amazing. The praise team was even more amazing than the other church I had visited.

The leader engaged the congregation.

She said things like, "Repeat after me. My God is an awesome God."

We repeated it back with the same energy and force in which she did.

Then she quoted scripture, "Clap your hands all ye people, shout unto God with a voice of triumph."

I kid you not, this praise team leader was something else. She was about six feet tall and wore high heels. And with every inch of her and from the depth of her soul, she ministered songs and led the congregation into a place I had never been before. That place was deep into the presence of God.

After the praise team filled the sanctuary with God's presence, it was time for a life-changing Word. This was the place where I learned about confessing the Word of God over my situations.

For example, when sickness or pain attacks my body, I confess God's healing word. In fact, before sickness appears I am to confess, "By His stripes I am healed."

They beat Jesus before going to the cross. Each of the thirty-nine stripes He took represents our healing from every sickness and disease.

One Sunday, after I returned home from church, Mom and I went out to get a burger. At that point she was still going to our old church, and as we ate she revealed to me that she had come away frustrated.

"I leave church feeling tired and empty," she said, "Everyone seems to get something out of service except me."

"I'm getting a lot out of this new church," I said, "and I think you will too. Why don't you come with me?"

She agreed, and from then on, on my Sundays off, Mom came with me and my cousin to the new church. Eventually, my aunt, my cousin's mother, came too. At the end of service, Mom and I would find a fast-food restaurant and talk about what we had experienced and how it was different from the old church.

"We are not getting these messages at our church," I told her. "We're not hearing about how to live as victorious Christians."

Her response was, "I don't want to leave my church. I shouldn't have to leave the church."

Although at that point I didn't push it any further, I knew I couldn't stay. I also knew I wouldn't leave my church without my mom, and at this point, she wasn't budging. She was ignoring the frustration that was meant to push her out of her comfort zone.

Have things gotten too comfortable for you? Are you miserable and frustrated, but afraid to change things? What's one step you can take? Who can you talk to who will listen without judgment? Are you ready for the next phase of your life?

CHAPTER

Seven

From Indecision to Decision

Aside from not wanting to leave my mother, I probably stayed at my old church longer than I should have because of indecision. I wanted to be one hundred percent sure that I was making the right decision. I wanted to make sure it was the right timing. Yet I was still unsure. In the meantime, I kept visiting the new church, and I kept praying. This would continue for years.

Finally, I decided the time was right. I turned in my resignation and just like that I was off to another world. I was leaving the place I had been all my life. I searched for the sweet spot. Here's to something new.

As soon as we started attending the church full time, a wonderful opportunity came up. The church made plans to attend a week-long spiritual conference in Ohio. Anybody who paid the fee could go. When they called the names of the preachers, Mom and I looked at each other in disbelief. People we had watched on television were going to be at this conference!

We were so excited. With every familiar name called out – names like Kenneth Copeland, Creflo Dollar, Rod Parsley, and many more - our smiles got bigger and bigger. We just knew we had to go to this conference. These were some of the people who had exposed me to the teaching of the Word. Now I would see them live and in person.

My cousin said, "I don't know some of these people, but since you are so excited I want to go too."

We drove from Georgia to Ohio on a big Greyhound bus. Our church van followed the bus. The van would take smaller groups, about fifteen people, to fun places and church services.

When the time for the conference finally came, my cousin and I were ready. Our clothes were all picked out, and we had note-books, pens, and Bibles. We were ready to receive more life-changing Word in our lives.

My cousin and I went to every meeting of the conference in that church van. On the way we chatted happily in anticipation of hearing another great Word. Most of the people wanted to see the big-name preachers. They normally preached at night. During the night services everybody went. They drove the big Greyhound bus.

It was a packed schedule. The first service started at ten a.m., then at lunchtime the van picked us up and took us back to the hotel. By two o'clock we were ready for the next service. Mom, who had also come to Ohio with us, started going with us too. When we found out there were places to buy food, we didn't bother returning to the hotel. We just stayed at the conference all day long.

It was a blast. We sang songs that our praise team sang with thousands of people. The presence of God filled the huge auditorium every single day. Most times we didn't have a clue who was preaching. We just took our notebooks out and took a lot of notes. We would compare those notes as we ate lunch after the meeting.

My cousin said, "Did you know we could be close to God even with thousands of people worshipping together? He knows how to reach me."

All too often we stay in a state of indecision, and it causes us to miss out on some unique adventures. Since we didn't move, we couldn't get what was behind the door. We kept wondering if it was good or bad. We haven't yet realized that just the act of deciding would put us closer to where we needed to be.

How long has indecision kept you stuck in the same place? How long have you been without peace? As you decide, peace settles the issue. If peace is there, go for it. I finally did. It was one of the best things I ever could have done.

Are you willing to pray and let go of worry and anxiety? Are you willing to receive His peace that passes all understanding Philippians 4:6-7? You may find it is one of the best things you can do for your life. What is one decision you can make this week that will get you moving forward?

Your decision could cause you to see and enter things you never thought possible. It could cause you to be in places you never dreamed about.

Many times, I had seen excerpts from the conference on TV, never imagining that I would one day be smack dab in the middle of it, worshiping with thousands of people, listening to the preachers who had first exposed me to the Word. This was God doing exceedingly, abundantly above all I could ask, think, or imagine (Ephesians 3:20).

Sometimes we stay on the surface of things. We haven't gone all-in. Even when we made steps, we did it halfheartedly. Now it's time to dive deep and go all in. All or nothing. Go big or go home.

Think about a time you needed to finish a school assignment or plan a vacation. Even if you did it at the last minute, you were all-in. What rewards came about as a result? Now think of times you did not go all-in. What rewards were withheld from you as a result of your indecision? Decide, and you will move closer to your sweet spot.

I went all-in at the conference. Every service, I was there. I soaked it in. I watched Matthew 6:33, the first verse Gloria, one of the people who exposed me to the Word of God, saw come to pass in my life. It reads, "Seek ye first the kingdom of God and His righteousness, and all these things will be added to you."

This passage held special significance for Gloria. Back when she didn't know much about God, she had gotten out the Bible given to her by her mother-in-law. On the first page her mother-in-law had written that verse, so it was the first verse she studied.

The truth of those words was now being played out in the conference. We weren't seeking experiences; they were added unto us as we sought God. And, as I sought Him, a ministry was born.

CHAPTER

To The Birth of a Ministry

One night during the conference, several people on the Greyhound bus decided they were hungry and wanted to stop and eat. The rest of us, including me, my mom, and my cousin disagreed because we didn't want to be late, but we were outvoted.

It seemed to take forever as we waited for all these people to order and eat their food in the restaurant while we waited on the bus.

Although we were way past upset and disappointed, we made the best out of an unpleasant situation by singing. Acts 16:25 talks about Paul and Silas. As mentioned earlier, they had been beaten and thrown into prison for preaching the Word of God. Yet at midnight they sang praises to God, and as a result everyone's chains were loosed.

It was midnight for us.

As we sang, I stopped and said, "Hey, we sound good together."

The others looked back at me and nodded in agreement. As we continued to sing on that Greyhound bus, our ministry was born. We started talking about a vision.

"What would you want our ministry to be like?" I asked.

My cousin replied, "I want to sing praise and worship music."

"Yes." Mom chimed in, and I agreed.

I also added, "It shouldn't just be about singing, but it should be a real ministry that can teach."

That night, while waiting for others to feed their bodies, God fed our souls by birthing our spiritual ministry. We believed God ordained the ministry of "The Anointed Sisters of Praise."

That night was full of favor. When we got to the conference, we discovered the auditorium was full, which meant we would have to go to the overflow room. We had never had to go to the over-flow room because we were always early.

Mom suggested a stop at the restroom, so we veered off from the crowd and headed there first.

When we came out of the restroom, favor was waiting for us. As we headed to the overflow room, an usher stopped us.

He said, "There are three seats inside the auditorium. Would you like to come in?"

We looked at each other and grinned from ear to ear.

In unison, we said yes, we gave the usher a heart-felt thank you.

That night, the praise and worship was, as we said in those days, "off the chain."

Gary Oliver, dressed in a long tuxedo coat with blue jeans, was playing the piano. Suddenly, he pushed the piano bench back, stood up, and sang from the depth of his soul. He put everything he had into the very last song, and as I sang to God along with him, I gave it everything I had as well.

Although I had heard him sing the song on TV, this time was different. I heard the changes in his voice. I saw the seriousness on his face. It connected with me in such a way that decades later, I remember, and it still stirs me up.

Instead of being angry that night, our spirits lifted. When we got back with our team who went to the overflow room, we were riding high from the service.

One person asked, "Where did you go?"

We responded to her, "We went to the restroom, and when we came out, an usher told us he had three seats and invited us in.

She replied, "Oh, I wish I was with you! It was cold and uncomfortable in the overflow room."

That night, as we got ready for bed, the three of us chatted about what the wonderful experience it had turned out to be. We were so excited we could hardly wait for the next day.

Sometimes we've gone no farther because we had no vision for it. We couldn't see past where we were. It didn't look possible, so we didn't even try. We didn't have anybody we could talk to who wouldn't laugh at our newfound desires.

Habakkuk 2:2 says, "Write the vision and make it plain."

Sometimes just having it in your head isn't enough. You must write it down so you can see it. You must talk about it with someone who is excited about you and for you.

On that big Greyhound bus, while waiting for others to finish eating in the restaurant, we were dreaming. We were dreaming of what could be. We were writing a vision and making it plain. We would eventually share that dream and vision with our pastor, our family, and ultimately, the world.

We would love to experience God's favor, but often we cannot dream or write a vision. We give into frustration or can't imagine how things might get better. But when we decide to move in the right direction, the favor of God shows up. We got great seats in the sanctuary. We experienced awesome praise and worship up close and personal. There is favor in the sweet spot.

Would you like to experience the favor of God in your life? Will you take time to see where you are now and where you want to be? Are you ready to write the vision and make it plain? Are you ready to find your sweet spot?

Will you dare to dream it's possible? Will you write the vision for your life, home, ministry, business, health, finances, et cetera? Will you share it with a trusted friend? Someone is on the other side waiting for you to find your sweet spot, so you can help them find theirs.

CHAPTER

Nine

To Watching the People

On one of our last days of the conference, we noticed something that disturbed us. Everyone waited for the doors of the conference to open and got frustrated. People we were with started singing and praising. They testified about how this conference blessed them.

The crowd outside felt better, but my cousin and I looked at each other in disbelief. If the conference had been all that, where were they when we were attending all the services? They were shopping and visiting the fun sites. It was disturbing. It made us wonder, is this the right place? I thought to myself, are these people *my* people?

Despite what I saw, I went back to the church. Yeah, I watched a little more closely and didn't take everything at face value. Although I kept watching, I kept going. I knew that place had what I needed. It had all started because I moved forward.

On that first Sunday after the trip, the praise team was on fire. They testified to the congregation about having a good time on the trip.

They shouted, "Hallelujah! Thank You, Jesus!"

Some waved their hands in agreement with what was being said. Some jumped up and down. Then they began the praise and worship service.

I was a little disappointed with them. The entire time they were speaking, shouting, and jumping, all I could do was watch.

I thought to myself, "Is this truly the right place for me? Or should I just get out of here as fast as I can?"

That feeling of distrust hindered me from deciding to join. Questions like, "Am I doing the right thing? Is this the right place? Would these feelings of doubt about the people go away?" were running through my mind.

Sometimes we've gone through disappointment that made us distrust people. We've had feelings of doubt that stopped us in our tracks.

We said, "If that's how they're going to be, I'll just leave them alone."

Then once again we're stuck in the same spot.

After coming this far are you willing to let the actions of others stop you? Will you move on despite what you see and hear? For we walk by faith, not by sight (2 Corinthians 5:7). What's one thing you can do despite what you've seen and heard?

Will you trust in the Lord with all your heart and lean not to your own understanding (Proverbs 3:5-6)? Will you allow God to direct your path? What's one thing you can do to move past distrust or disappointment?

John 16:33 says, "These things I have spoken unto you that in Me you may find peace. In the world you will have tribulation, but be of good cheer for I have overcome the world."

When I first saw and heard the people at the new church, I had put them on a pedestal.

I remember thinking, *Wow look at them. They have got it together.* I wanted to be like them. We all wanted the same thing: revelation of God. Now, as I observed them and saw their actions and heard their conversations, I realized they were just regular people with issues.

We've all gotten to places and found out things weren't as we expected. Many of our disappointments have caused us to turn back in fear or refuse to let others in. In order to find a sweet spot, we've got to take a chance. We've got to deal with people and our trust issues.

Have you let past hurts and disappointment hold you back or keep you stuck? Do you want to get out of that pattern? What's one thing you can do to move past the hurt and disappointment?

I watched my situation closely and prayed continuously. As a result, God gave me a revelation. It was an "aha" moment. People are just people. We all have issues, whether with God or not. They were doing the best they could with the revelation of God they had, and so was I.

God wants to reveal to you how to move past hurt and disappointment. Matthew 6:33, "Seek first the kingdom of God and His righteousness and all these things shall be added onto you."

CHAPTER

Ten

To "It Seems to Be a Good Fit."

Do you remember getting ready for school to start and getting everything in order? For me, one of those things was buying shoes. I remember going up and down the long aisle of shoe boxes, looking for my size – six and a half. When I found it, I looked up and down those shelves for the style I liked, then tried them on to measure where my toes were. It was only after I walked around in them that I knew they were a good fit; that's when I finally carried the shoes to the register.

Now I was doing the same thing with church. First, I visited this church while still attending my church. It was like going up and down the aisle trying to find that six and a half. Then I left my church and visited this church all the time. It was like looking at the six-and-a-half shelf for the right style. Then I traveled with them out of state to a conference. It was like trying on the shoe. I had to try it on and see if it fit. Being disappointed and watching the people were the times of measuring where my toes and ankles were. As I continued going to the church and getting a revelation, I was walking around to see if it was a good fit.

Then why hadn't I joined the church yet? Why hadn't I bought the shoes?

I wanted something different. I wanted to be at a church that had a praise service and the Word taught. I just didn't know whether I had found the right spot. I kept going and taking notes. I enjoyed this new experience. This is what I wanted. This is what I needed.

Yet I still felt stuck. Before I had felt stuck at my old church because I liked certain aspects of it. In some ways, things were good. I didn't want to leave my friends and family. However the need to be taught the Word in a different way was more important.

Now, I was visiting the new church; I was tithing, and giving offerings, yet I had not been able to bring myself to join. In my mind, to leave my old church was one thing. In my mind, to join another church meant I had no possibility of ever going back.

In 1 Kings 18, Elijah asked the people, "How long will you halt between two opinions? If God be God, serve Him. If Baal, serve him." The people answered him not a word. It seems that, like me, they were also unable to decide!

Are you willing to be delivered from being stuck? Are you ready to make some decisions so you can get what you've been exposed to? Why are you stuck? What decision or decisions do you need to make to be free from being stuck?

Since I wanted to be delivered from being stuck, one day before entering the church, I turned to my mom and cousin and asked, "Do you want to join today?"

Their response was yes.

That day, along with my mom and cousin, I got all God had for me. It was the day I decided not to let indecision keep me stuck. It was an exciting and awesome day. The entire congregation seemed to be happy that we took that step of faith.

I remember we were not in the back of the church. We were somewhere in the middle. I remember walking down the aisle, how it wasn't that long but seemed to take forever. My heart beat faster and faster, then calmed down as I looked down into the smiling faces of those around me. Also, hearing the church clapping and confirming us was awesome.

What surprises me about questions is they can locate where a person is. After Adam and Eve sinned by eating the fruit from the tree, they hid. Although they knew they were not to eat from that tree, they gave into their temptation.

God asked a question, "Adam, where are you?"

Adam started off good. And he said, "I heard thy voice in the garden, and I was afraid, because I was naked; and I hid myself." (Genesis 3:10)

Adam located himself as being afraid and naked. Then Adam wouldn't take full responsibility for his actions. He blamed the woman that God had given him.

Then the woman blamed the serpent.

They wouldn't be honest and locate themselves. As long as they were blaming someone else for what they did or where they were, they couldn't properly locate themselves. We often do the same things, saying, "It's not my fault" or "The devil made me do it."

All the while God is asking, "Where are you?"

Where was I? For months I had visited this church with my mom and cousin and her mom. I enjoyed the praise and worship and the Word of God. I was learning. I was excited. Yet I failed to locate myself and make a commitment. I was still stuck.

One idea, one thought, gave me the opportunity to locate myself. *Do you want to join today?* That question got me out of my seat, down the aisle, and into the church as a member. In locating myself and where I was and where I wanted to be, I made a commitment. That commitment freed me up in ways I could never have imagined.

Where are you? Where do you want to be? Are you willing to commit? Go for it. Why should you continue to be stuck when God has so much in store for you?

PART 2

MOVING FORWARD

CHAPTER

Eleven

To Stop Playing It Safe

Once we finally quit playing it safe, we not only joined the new church, we got involved. My mom and cousin became greeters, and they were great at it. I took a different path. I worked with the children's church in the music department.

When I worked with the music ministry at my old church, I had help from directors; but this time I was on my own. During Bible Study I taught songs to the kids between the ages of six and twelve years old.

On Sundays I went to church for prayer and praise service. After the praise service ended, I would head to the children's church, where we held our own praise service, which included chanting and singing, before returning to the main building to hear the sermon for the day.

Well, talk about growth and doing something new! I got involved with the teen ministry. Leslie V, the quiet one who would like to stay in the background, joined the step team. I'll talk more about step teams later on. Although I had seen college step teams, I had never stepped myself, so I was shocked by how quickly and easily I learned.

When the leader of the team asked if I would like to help teach the steps, I didn't hesitate. Now I was not only learning something new, I was sharing my new skill with others. The leader and I worked well together – she taught the faster learners; I watched and taught the slower learners at a pace they could keep up with. Our step team was pretty tight, and to this day I wish we had taken videos of it.

As the step team faded out, I turned toward the music department. That didn't go too well. All I can say is that was definitely *not* the sweet spot.

Sometimes we get to a place and never give back. We just take and take. We sit in the back and listen, yet we never get involved. We just complain about this and that.

Do like I did. I got to the place and got active. I did my part. We all have a part to play at the place where God is sending us.

Are you ready to take your place? Are you ready to do you and give back to the people and places that are helping you?

CHAPTER

Twelve

Moving into Rejection

If you were alive in the seventies or eighties, you probably remember the hit comedy show, *The Jeffersons.* Not only was it very funny, it also had a great theme song that captured the show perfectly. The Jefferson family had come from poor beginnings, but they kept going, despite the obstacles, and finally got "a piece of the pie."

While the song played, you could see them move. You saw the big moving van. You saw Louise crying in the cab because she was moving away from her friend Edith. You saw them in the elevator, riding up toward the top of a luxury high-rise. You saw the new apartment, new friends, and new neighbors. They moved upward. There would be more adventures in store for them.

That's what happened to me. I moved from my old church, my family, and my friends. I moved because God exposed me to something different. I moved because I wanted and needed something new. Just like in the Jeffersons, that was not the end of the story. There would be more adventures in store for me, too.

When we first made the commitment to join the church, things were good. The praise and worship continued to set the atmosphere. The life-changing Word still made me think.

In the beginning of creation, the world was dark and empty (Genesis 1:2). In the first section of the chapter, the same phrase repeats: "And God said." It was the Word that God spoke that turned the world from dark and empty to bright and full. It was the Word that turned things around in the beginning. It was turning my life around now.

Of course, my intention with this new church was to learn and grow, but something happened. At first I did not notice it. With the level of Word that was taught, the church grew. It grew a lot on a back road in the middle of nowhere. This reminded me of the teaching from John the Baptist. He had a Word from God that was so simple and so good.

"Repent, for the kingdom of heaven is at hand."

People wanted and needed that message so much, they went out into the wilderness to get it.

In the same way those people came to hear John the Baptist, they came to hear the Word at my church. As a church group, we looked for a location in the city where more people would come and join. And they did. Every Sunday, it seemed more and more people showed up.

As our church grew, cliques formed. I found myself not "in" with the "in" crowd, but "out" with the "out" crowd.

I remembered opening the door of the church and walking into the foyer. It was the first time I had ever heard of a hallway being called a foyer. It had clean white floors. As you looked towards the ceiling, there was a chandelier in which the lights flowed downward and brightened the entire area with its intense light.

On the right was a long desk. It was deep brown and looked like a display in a jewelry store. After service, people could come to the desk and point to a book or CD they wanted to purchase. They could buy whatever they wanted at that desk.

As I walked into the foyer, two people from the "in" crowd were talking to each other. When they looked at the door and saw me, they went back to talking to each other. Just as in high school, they didn't even say hi. With everything I could muster, I walked bravely and boldly past them with a smile on my face. I returned the favor by not saying hi to them either.

I knew I didn't fit with them. I knew I wasn't in the "in" crowd. I knew they didn't like me. Of course, those kinds of things make a normal person get out and run in the other direction. I never would have imagined they would reject me at church.

Some, when they experience rejection, hightail it out of there. *See ya, wouldn't want to be ya. Hasta la vista, baby.* They let hurt and disappointment hinder them from finding the sweet spot.

How have you allowed the rejection of others to stop you from moving forward? Are you willing to talk to God about the rejection you have experienced in life? Will you allow rejection by others to stop you? What is one thing you can do to release these emotions of rejection? Rejection will not allow you to flow in the sweet spot. Forgiveness is a step that moves you closer to your sweet spot.

CHAPTER

Thirteen

To Keep Going Despite Rejection

Despite the rejection I experienced, I faithfully attended service every Sunday and Wednesday. I followed Jesus, and I determined there was no turning back. I enjoyed the Word and the praise team. I just kept going.

And because I kept going, I found sweet spots. I did things I never thought I could do. It had been a while since I had worked with children, but I got in there and did my best. The children were eager to learn and eager to please.

One song I taught the kids was "The 10 Commandments," which was sung to the tune of "The Farmer in the Dell." Commandment number ten was "Be content with what you have," They sang it with all their hearts and enjoyed themselves. They called me Miss Leslie. They accepted me as I was.

As I mentioned earlier, I was also asked to take part in the step ministry for the teens. Though I had seen the shows in college I had never taken part because only the sororities and fraternities did that sort of thing. Back then, the teams were identified by their colors; for example the Alpha Phi Alpha fraternity's colors were black and gold, so that's what they wore during their shows.

Step shows were fun to watch. I remember one particular routine by the Alphas. They stood in three lines, upright and at attention. Their elbows were out, their fists were together at the front of their chest as they awaited the leader's command. Then the show was on. They had the same black boots, which they stomped on the ground to make the beat. They did every step in unison, whether the team had five members or fifteen.

Then started clapping to the beat as well. Some clapped through their legs and on their knees. They continued to step to the beat.

Then one section broke out with a distinct step, doing something different with their hands and feet. This group kept this rhythm as the next group started another beat with their hands and feet.

At the conclusion of this step, the team gave out their fraternity shout. Then they resumed the upright position they'd had at the beginning. It was truly an outstanding performance. The crowd roared in awe and amazement at what they had just witnessed.

Of course, that had been many years ago. I hadn't been to a step show since, and I had never even heard of a church step team. Curious, I attended the first meeting, learned a few steps, and before I knew it I had joined the team. Over time, I formed a bond with Lisa, the team leader. One day she surprised me by asking if I would help her teach the steps. It was a neat experience, and one I will treasure forever.

My point is, had I not kept going because of the rejection, I never would have been a stepper. I never would have this adventure. The team didn't even exist until after the rejection. The team didn't exist until I kept going. In the sweet spot, things come out of you. I never knew I could do this, but in the sweet spot I found out that I could. God can open doors no man can shut. He opened that door for me but I had to walk through it. It was an amazing time in my life.

We don't know what's in us. We don't know what can come out of us or from us. If we stay where we are, we may never know. Those gifts, talents, skills, and abilities may not be needed where we are. It's only in the sweet spot that things can come out of us and from us.

Do you believe there are gifts, talents, skills, and abilities inside of you? Do you believe certain places or spots are more suitable for certain gifts? Although I don't know a lot about fishing, I have heard certain spots are best to catch certain types of fish. Also, it takes a certain bait to catch a certain fish.

In the same way, there are certain spots that go with your particular gifts. In this way, you can do what God has called you to do. There are certain people you're called to "catch," or help.

What's one thing you can do to make sure you're at the right place? Will you make a list of things you know are your gifts?

The team rehearsed on Saturday mornings. When the team showed up we couldn't help but laugh. I'm about five feet and Lisa was just a little taller than that. We would be teaching the steps to teenagers that towered over us.

Lisa would show the team each new step then the others followed her lead. I watched for those who were struggling and couldn't catch on as fast. I worked with them.

As I worked the slower steppers, I constantly encouraged them. "You almost got it. Let's try it again." I kept breaking it down and showing the steps over and over again. When they got frustrated, I just kept encouraging them. "You can do it." When they did the steps correctly, there were high fives all around. Now we were a solid step team.

If I had been paying attention, I would have noticed more about my gifts. Now, looking back at it, I see teaching was a gift. I taught voice parts to choirs and Bible study and stepping to teenagers. The other gift I have is that of encouragement. I cheered them on, literally every "step" of the way. It came out because I was in the sweet spot.

CHAPTER

Fourteen

To Keep Moving Despite Being Ignored

Recall that when we went to the conference, my mom, cousin and I were led to the birth of a ministry, "The Anointed Sisters of Praise." Before the church moved to its new sanctuary, we had some opportunity to sing. First, though, I had to talk to the minister of music about it.

"What is your name?" he asked me.

I responded, "The Anointed Sisters of Praise."

"Are you anointed?"

Without missing a beat, I replied "Yes."

So we set it up. We were to sing at church on Sunday. We all bought black and white shirts so we looked the same. We each wore black pants and a black suit jacket with black heels.

When they called our name, we got up and went to the front of the church. Mom did her call to worship.

"Come on, everybody, let's praise a little. For He is worthy of praise."

As she exhorted the people, we stood confidently behind her, as if we had been doing this all our lives. We hadn't – this was our first time – but we had rehearsed. We were ready.

We sang a cappella in three-part harmony. I sang soprano, my cousin sang alto, and my mom sang tenor. Our fast song got the people upon their feet. They were clapping and singing along. Our slow song invited people to lift their hands to the king of kings and worship. It was a success.

Sometimes we've done something new and nailed it. At other times, we've done something new and it flopped. We paid so much attention to the flop that we failed to try again. We felt stuck.

Are you willing to be stuck in the same place repeatedly year after year, month after month, week after week, day after day? Or are you ready to find your sweet spot? What's one new thing you can do? What are you willing to do?

I was moving. I was getting songs together and teaching voice parts. I was finding my sweet spot with this new thing. I didn't even know it.

The thing to realize is an enemy who doesn't want us to find the sweet spot exists. In the sweet spot, we bear fruit. It's fruit that will benefit people and the kingdom of God. The fruit shows up little by little. Mark 4:28 says, "First the blade, then the ear, and then the full corn in the ear."

The enemy puts obstacles in the way. After John baptized Jesus, the Spirit led Him into the wilderness to be tempted by the devil for forty days and forty nights. During that temptation, Jesus won at every turn. Now it was my time.

After we moved into a new sanctuary, things changed, or at least things that had been hidden were now being brought into the light. Although the people loved the ministry of The Anointed Sisters of Praise, the "in" crowd was in charge. Our opportunities to sing became fewer and fewer.

Iris didn't care about the "in" crowd. She was nice, sweet, and funny. She spoke to everybody, whether they had a title or not. God blessed her to write and direct plays, which she did every year. She asked our ministry to sing in her plays at church, and once again we were a success. Even though people rejected us and ignored our ministry at church, we still got invited to sing.

Often people ignore us or reject us and it hurts so badly we give up. We become stuck in the same spot. We don't realize that this is actually coming from the enemy.

Are you ready to get unstuck? Are you willing to move past being ignored, rejected, and hurt? What's one area where you feel stuck? What is one thing you can do to get unstuck and find your sweet spot?

It only takes one step to begin a movement. We had little opportunity to minister or serve at church, but my cousin had a heart for people.

She said, "I know some people we can help. We can go into their homes and minister to them."

Mom and I agreed, so we went.

I remember one particular home we went to. The mom had kids who were always sick with something. Upon our arrival, my cousin introduced us and chatted, then we started singing. Afterwards, I taught from the Bible about healing. While the teaching revelation flowed out of my mouth, the mom received it. We prayed for her children and her house.

The next week, the mom told my cousin, "I know y'all have something because I could feel it. Also, my kids are doing well."

I don't know if you picked up on this or not, but the gift of teaching showed up again. First, I taught voice parts. Despite rejection, I taught new songs to the kids. Then I taught teenagers to step. Now, I was teaching in people's homes and eventually in the nursing home.

Sometimes we've showed up and people rejected or ignored us. Sometimes people didn't take time to find out what was in us or what we offered. Sometimes we didn't know ourselves.

Even if they rejected you or ignored you in the past, are you willing to move forward? What's one step you can take?

I realized that when I went to use the outside places like the nursing homes, the gifts flowed even more.

You too can find one step to take. You too can continue. You can see things flowing out you never knew you had. When you're in a sweet spot, that's what happens.

Remember, God is no respecter of persons (Acts 10:34). If He did it for me, He can do it for you. He's doing it for me right now. Will you trust He can do it for you too?

CHAPTER

To Being Lied to and Hurt

As time went on I continued to enjoy most things about the church. The step ministry was fun but eventually broke up. That was okay, though. I was there first and foremost to get the Word, and that's what I got. I took lots of notes. I enjoyed praise and worship.

Wow! After struggling for so long about whether to join the church, I finally found what I was looking for. More struggles, like being rejected by the "in" crowd, ensued, but we overcame each step. We were growing. All was well, or so we thought.

Then, out of nowhere, a rumor started going around the city, with people saying, "Did you hear? Did you hear? Girl, let me tell you what I heard."

Sunday rolled in, people came again to see what the pastor would say.

He preached a sermon on "Staying with the Ship." He recounted the story of the Apostle Paul, who was on a ship that was headed for a wreck. Many people felt they needed to get off the ship (Acts 27:27-32), but the Word of God came to Paul to stay with the ship. That was the only way to save their lives.

Of course you and I know it makes little sense to stay on a sinking ship. Even when the Titanic sank, those who could get out got out to safety. When God says stay with the ship, that's what you do. That's what my pastor was trying to get through to the congregation.

I was so disappointed in him and by him, and though I stayed all the way through the service I couldn't even look up at him. I just kept looking down at my Bible or at other members of the congregation. Some were fidgeting; they were ready for the sermon to be over, too. They were ready for the announcement to be made.

Shortly after the sermon, it was time for the announcement. The pastor stood up and spoke to the congregation.

He said, "To the congregation and friends in this congregation, you may have heard... And also you may have heard... Blah blah blah..." Then he started talking to us about staying with the ship."

What?! That's it?! Do you call that an apology?!

I never once heard the words, "I'm sorry."

I never once heard, "I was wrong."

I didn't even hear, "I made a mistake."

I only heard, "You might have heard..."

I wanted to say, "Yes, I heard it, but I expected you to own up to it. I expected you to do as you preached. I expected you to tell me the truth. Then we could have gotten past it. Then we could have grown, but you never did."

Before that happened, no matter what criticism people had to say about my pastor, I always took up for him.

I said, "Well, the reason our church is doing this or that is because we're growing into a new level."

Everything he told me from the pulpit, I told his critics. I would have stayed with the ship too, but I felt betrayed. I had the sinking feeling of being lied to repeatedly for years.

Now I knew why I wasn't in with the "in-crowd." They all knew the pastor wasn't living what he was preaching. They all knew because they were hanging out with him. They knew. They knew.

I talked to God and told Him I was sad. Of course He already knew, and He was working in me to will and to do of His good pleasure (Philippians 2:13).

When the following Friday arrived, I thought to myself. Hey, I don't feel sad anymore. I don't know how. I don't know when God did it, but He had removed my hurt.

Of course, I still remembered what happened. I still remembered the unfairness of it all. I still remembered how I felt. However, it no longer ruled over me. I still believed God had sent me to that church.

While I was at that place, I grew. I didn't know the Word before this church. I didn't know where books were in the Bible. This church gave me a good foundation of the Word. Gifts, skills, and talents came out of me. I never knew these things were in me. These things learned at this place helped me help others even now. I have no regrets about this place.

Yes, there were many times I said I wished I knew from the beginning that this was going to happen. Of course I said that, because if I had known I wouldn't have joined. I would have run away as fast as Forest Gump. Run Leslie Run.

Now I understood what the old folks meant when they said things like, "I wouldn't take nothing for my journey."

Neither would I. Had I not gone through this, I couldn't help or encourage others.

Sometimes we go through unfair situations. We think everything was okay, then out of nowhere the shoe dropped and ugly truths were exposed. It revealed the lie that left us deflated, sad, hurt, disappointed, confused, and angry. What do we do now?

Those unfair situations have kept you stuck for far too long. Holding on to things has hardened you from finding your sweet spot. How long will you go around the same mountain repeatedly? Are you ready to put the past behind you? Are you willing to talk to God about your present and past hurts? Hurt people hurt people. Are you ready to forgive these people? Are you ready to let it go so you can get to your sweet spot?

CHAPTER

Sixteen

To Breaking Ties

Just because God heals you from a situation doesn't mean you have to stay. Here I was again. Mom wasn't going with me to this church anymore, and I knew it was time for me to leave as well. I didn't want to be associated with this place of bad morals, corrupt good manners (1Corinthians 15:33.), only unlike last time, I now had nowhere to go.

We've all been in situations where we knew things would not change or get better. We're then faced with the decision to stay or leave.

What are you going to do? Is there a situation in your life where the decision to stay or go is mandatory? If you're in a relationship where you are getting beat up every day, I suggest you, "run, Forrest, run." But I can't make that decision for you; you need to do that for yourself. Aren't you tired of being sick and tired?

Immediately, Mom and I went to explore other churches. The next place we went to had a pretty good praise team. The pastor of the church did a good job. I took a lot of notes. We started going on Wednesdays too. It was good.

One thing that was different about it from the church we'd left was acceptance. These people at that church accepted us as we were. They wanted a mixed congregation. They wanted us to join. It was nice to be wanted for a change.

I remember one time walking into the church. We came in through the glass double doors. We walked down the hall, where people greeted us with smiles and hugs.

"Hello, how are you doing today? Enjoy the service." They sincerely said these things from their hearts.

As Mom and I entered the sanctuary, I saw the pastor talking to someone. My first thought was to walk past them and let them finish their conversation. The reason I did this was because that's all I knew.

I was in for a wonderful surprise. The pastor stepped away from the person he was talking to and blocked our path.

He took the time to say, "Hi, how are you doing?"

We replied in unison, "Fine."

He also took the time to hug us both before going back to his conversation.

On the way home from church that night, we had a mixture of excitement and sadness.

Mom said, "Wasn't it something that the pastor stopped his conversation just to speak to us?"

I said, "Yes, that's pretty exciting to be accepted and loved as you are. It is sad that small action would make us feel like that."

What I meant was we didn't get that from where we had come from.

People rejected or ignored us. People accepted and appreciated us. A lot of times we've dealt with rejection for so long, we don't know how to receive love.

It's time to break free from ties that bind. He who the Son sets free is free indeed (John 8:36). It's time to form relationships with people who want the best for you. It's time to be with people who believe the best in you and for you. It's time to do that for others. We can also find good relationships in a sweet spot if you let them.

Break ties with past hurts and lies. Move forward. Are you ready? Forgetting those things that are behind and pressing toward the mark for the prize of the high calling, which is in Christ Jesus (Philippians 3:12-14)

One day while I was at work, my cousin called. Of course, I was always glad to hear from her.

I said, "What's up?"

She said, "I am no longer a member of the church."

"Really?" I replied, surprised because she had decided to stay when Mom and I left.

"Yes, I was talking to someone who knows about the situation."

She went on to say that after his so-called "apology," he turned around that same night and kept doing what he had been doing.

I replied, "What a shame. Good for you."

I couldn't wait to tell Mom. We were happy at the third church we were visiting. Once again, we had opportunities to go places. We were also thrilled to learn that Pastor Rod Parsley, who had hosted that conference in Ohio, was the spiritual father of the pastor of this church; therefore the pastor tried to run his ministry the same way. Pastor Parsley often met with his spiritual sons and gave them advice and encouragement.

And since these spiritual sons also supported each other, once again we got to travel. One trip we took with this church was to Atlanta. This program featured Pastor Parsley's mother. She was a little fireball! Just a bit taller than me, she spoke boldly, confidently, and with assurance. She spoke with conviction and power.

She impressed me. She seemed to portray all the qualities I didn't have. Even then I believed God was dropping into my spirit something new. I believed He was exposing me to what I could be. I missed it back then, but I see it clearly now.

God doesn't want us to remain in the same spot. He gently exposes us to new things so we can get new ideas and dreams. So often we miss it.

For a while, Mom and I were happy visiting the new church. We went every Sunday and Wednesday because that was what we were used to doing. Then the pastor started talking more and more about us joining. He said he had made new rules for the congregation.

We had just left a bunch of crap. We were not ready to jump into anything. And since I knew the pastor was pushing for commitment, we left.

No matter what it may seem like to someone else, you're the only one who knows what you're ready for. Even if it means disappointing someone else, it's better to do what's right for you than to accommodate someone else's wishes. Even though it may make no sense, you must follow your heart.

Often we get mad at people for where we are in our lives. We did not realize that the choice was always up to us. Sometimes people mean well and are just trying to push us the way they think we should go.

There's a time and a season for everything under the sun (Ecclesiastes 3:1).

In the sweet spot at this place, I learned. I saw new things and more things. I saw the possibility of what could be. It just wasn't the place for me to be forever. It was a necessary step on the journey to the ultimate sweet spot.

Sometimes we go to good places and settle there. In the Bible, we hear a lot about Abraham. In Genesis 11:31, Terah set out from Ur of the Chaldean to go to Canaan. When Terah and his family came to Haran, they settled there. I don't think Terah was supposed to settle in Haran.

When God talked to Abraham, he was still in Haran. His father, Terah, died in Haran. God spoke to Abraham to lead him out to go to the land of Canaan.

Are you ready to put off the old things and put on the new? Are you ready to let go of the rejection from others? Are you willing to receive the love? Where is one place you're accepted and loved? What can you do to get around and stay around those people?

Are you willing to reflect on your life to see where you exposed yourself to new things, new people, or new jobs? Behold, God will do a new thing (Isaiah 43:19). Are you willing to look and see things God exposed you to? Did you run with it? Are you doing it now? Would you like to? What's one step you can do concerning the things God has exposed you to?

Have you settled for less than God's best? Have you settled for "good" or "better" when you could have had the best? Have you allowed people to push you toward things you were not ready to commit to? Are there places in your life where God has given you a glimpse that there is more? Are you willing to move out of Haran into your Canaan? What's one decision that could move you to the best God has for you?

What are you going to do? Is there a situation in your life where the decision to stay or go is mandatory?

CHAPTER

Seventeen

To Beginning Again and Splitting

Once again Mom and I found ourselves without a church. It was time to begin again, and my cousin had left church number two, we could begin again together. It was just like old times, except this time we better understood what we were looking for. This time when it didn't feel right, we knew to leave.

We didn't give up; we kept going.

I would ask, "How about trying this place? "

We went.

Then my cousin had been listening to this person and liked him.

She asked, "What about this place?" So we went.

It was a nice building. When we walked into the church, I looked up at their choir stand. It impressed me. Steps covered in a blue carpet that led to the musicians. The keyboardist played anything with ease. His drummer played right in beat with him. They played before service began.

Then the praise team walked boldly and confidently to their places. The keyboardist played music based on the leader exhorting the praise. It was awesome.

Then they opened their mouths and sang boldly and confidently, all in the same tune. By now you remember I loved harmony. I never could stand unison unless it flowed back and forth from unison to harmony. That was strike one.

As praise and worship continued, things got better. They set up to enter God's presence. Then the praise team leader screamed through the microphone.

"Kids, stop playing in the presence of God!"

When she said that, it jerked me. I looked up at her. I saw the stern look on her face. It was over for me. Although she kept singing, it troubled me. That was strike two.

When the pastor got up, I was still upset by what the praise leader had done. I had not entered into God's Presence. I honestly couldn't hear what the pastor said. That was strike three. I was uncomfortable and was ready to get out of there.

My cousin, on the other hand, loved it. She already watched the pastor on TV and knew she enjoyed him. She eventually joined that church while Mom and I continued to look for our spot.

The ministry, as we knew it, had ended. This made me afraid because my cousin and I were moving in different directions in other areas of our lives as well.

I was so sad because we were not just cousins; we were friends, and had been since I was eleven years old. Until that time I had thought I was the youngest granddaughter. What I didn't know was that one of my uncles had children I had never met, including a daughter who was a year and a half younger than me. His sisters, my aunts, told him he needed to bring his children around so we could get to know them. He listened to them and brought his kids over. His son went with the boys. His daughter stayed inside with me. I have always been rather quiet and shy. I always found it hard to talk to new people. But that was not the case with her.

The first time we met each other we said, "Hi."

Next thing we knew, it was hours later.

Her dad said, "It's time to go. We have been here all day long."

"Really," I said.

Then I looked up at the black digital clock by grandma's bed. I realized by those bright red numbers on the clock that my uncle was right. It only felt like a few minutes had passed. It only took a second to connect.

Now I was sad because I felt like I had lost my friend forever.

Although we had split up, I reached out to her. I was nervous. I didn't know how it would turn out. I hadn't heard from her. Maybe she was mad at me. Maybe we were really over. I pushed past the fear and called her.

"Hello, I know your birthday is around the corner. I know it's a normal custom to go out to eat. Do you want to go to lunch with me?"

I had a silent sigh of relief as I waited for her response. My part was over. Now it was her turn.

She excitedly replied, "Yes!"

We met up again for the first time after the split. We hugged each other. I gave her my gift. We sat down at the restaurant and talked and talked and talked. It was just like old times. I was happy. Although it felt like only a few minutes, hours had passed.

We often make shifts and changes in our lives. Sometimes we let people and places go that no longer serve us.

We say things like, "Let's keep in touch," but we don't.

We never think about the fact that God put us in places for a season, for a reason. In every place He puts us, people are there for relationships to be established. Some relationships are worth fighting for.

Although we were going in different directions, I still had a connection with my cousin that I didn't want to lose. So I mustered up the courage and reached out. My situation turned out well.

Although we don't get together often, every time we get together we talk and talk and talk. We still feel like it's only been a few minutes when hours have passed.

Have you let relationships go that were worth saving? Have you ever been in a relationship where the "season" was over, but the relationship was not? Is there someone you can reach out to or connect with? Are you willing to pray and seek God?

If it's over, let it go. If it's worth saving, go for it.

CHAPTER

Eighteen

To Something Really Different

Mom and I kept searching, but nothing seemed to be the right place. One day out of the blue, I got an email from a big church I watched on TV. The pastor was starting a satellite church in my city.

What did that mean? Well, the email showed me the meeting place was at the local movie theater. A praise team would come in. We would watch a pre-recorded sermon. Eventually service would stream live directly to the church.

That email disturbed me. It excited me for a church that taught the Word in my city. I was excited that I wouldn't have to drive far. However, a church on a screen didn't sit right with me. I couldn't wrap my mind around a church like this.

It helped that I knew the pastor, and that he knew about the situation at the second church. You see, the pastor of that second church had been a spiritual son to this pastor. So this pastor knew members were leaving. He knew they were like me and needed somewhere to go. He provided a solution just for us.

Although it was a strange solution, Mom and I went and tried it out. I drove to the parking lot of the movie theater. I walked up to the place where we purchased tickets.

I said to the lady through the window, "I am here for the church service."

She smiled and said, "Come on in."

Once inside, an usher showed us which way to go. My heart beat fast as we walked down the hall and into the place. We grabbed a seat in the back.

To our surprise, we saw others from the second church here too. We saw people we knew had the same skepticism we had. We saw our familiar church people. They were also trying to find a place to belong. They were there for the same reasons we were.

I loved it. The praise team was impressive. In fact, my second church had patterned its praise team after this one. It amazed me that even in a movie theater, we felt God's presence.

The sermon was on Genesis 12. At the beginning of this chapter, God spoke to Abraham about leaving his family. God told Abraham that as he stepped out, He would show Abraham where to go.

I wrote a lot of notes that day. I was excited about the Word. I understood it.

I told Mom, "This is just like us. We left our family. Now we have left another church family. It's like God was reassuring us to step out. He would lead us."

Mom's response was, "Do you want to go back again next week?"

I did. Now we had somewhere to go.

Finally, the time came for us to move out of the movie theater into our own church building. We rented from a church who had outgrown the building. It was a brick building like the church I grew up in.

It had about ten steps that led to the porch. This porch was wider and longer. When it rained, the overhead covering protected us. When we walked into the building, the first thing we saw were pews. A row on the right and left, just like my old church.

Like always, I went to church faithfully every Sunday and Wednesday, but didn't join right away. I was content and happy with things as they were. Then one day a minister came from Atlanta with a charge.

He said, "You've been coming to this church week after week. Some have been coming for months. This is your church. If you believe this is your church, join. If you join, get involved. Do something. Don't just take and take from the ministry. Give back."

This minister came with a heart for the people. Although he was a preacher, he didn't sound pushy or bossy.

He spoke with compassion and love for the people. He spoke with conviction about how this ministry had changed his life. He spoke because he knew if we connected with the ministry, our lives would change too.

It resonated with me. I connected with him and what he spoke. I knew it was time for me to commit.

Shortly after this minister visited, Mom and I joined the church and got connected. Someone volunteered us to work on a project, one I never would have picked for myself. Once a month our church planned some type of meal with a theme. Mom and I helped with the kitchen duties. On those Sundays, people brought whatever they signed up to bring. We treated them warmly.

I had never worked in the kitchen before that time. Normally I just fixed a plate and ate. Now I was learning to do something different.

We had an excellent leader. I did not frustrate her as I tried to get tablecloths on a long, brown plain table. She taught me to take a napkin and roll the silverware into the napkin. Wow, it looked pretty. I did that.

She said, "Yeah, that's right. That's good."

When I got comfortable, she left me to finish my project. I arranged tablecloths, silverware and napkins. I continued from one table to the next until the tables in the room were complete.

The rest of the team warmed the cold food. They fixed the room to make it look like a banquet area.

I carried long, gray pans down the hall. We put some water in the pans and lit the fire underneath. Then we put the food into another grey pan and placed it above the other pan. For the final touch, I placed the big spoons in the grey pans.

When church was over, the people came. We served them piping hot food.

Until I opened my mouth and asked, "Do you want green beans or mashed potatoes? "

I didn't know I had a natural gift for that. When the people came through the line, I helped serve the people. I talked with them. I watched to see if food was getting low. If it was, I walked to the kitchen to let people know I needed another pan.

For an introvert that often stayed to herself, that was a breakthrough. Another hidden gift I didn't know I had came out. I liked it. Not only did I communicate well with people in line, I communicated well with the team.

As the people ate and got full, cleanup began for the team. Mom washed dishes so we could return dishes to those who had lent them to the church. Some dishes belonged to the church, and Mom put them up in their rightful places.

While she did that, I folded up the tablecloths. Some tablecloths I saved for later. Some I threw away. I brought serving spoons to the kitchen to be washed. I put chairs and tables back to their rightful places. I fixed us to go boxes so we could take food home and enjoy the meal for ourselves. It was over, but it felt good.

The minister was right. As I committed to the church and joined. I noticed I had changed. As I committed and joined this church, opportunities came. Gifts shined through that I never knew I had. These gifts came out of me because I committed to serve.

Often we've been in places, but never committed. We've been with people but never committed. However, we will never rise and stick with anything without making a commitment. Without commitment, we have run at the first sign of trouble or we had a Plan B.

Are you ready to go all-in? Are you ready to join that group or begin again? What's one thing you can commit to? Maybe it's a project that needs to be done. Where can you serve now? Who can you help now? There is no telling what gifts will come naturally flowing out of you.

If you would like the entire workbook, click the link www. findyoursweetspotseries.com/resources

Nineteen

To Another Commitment

As I got busy serving in this department, another opportunity came up: to become involved with the praise team. As with any new opportunity, fear rose. This time it was because I would have to audition. In my previous churches, if you wanted to sing, you joined the choir and that was it.

If I knew I could sing, why was I worried, anxious, and fretting about an audition? It was unknown territory. I'd never done it before. What if I auditioned, and they told me, "You're not good enough?"

Church people had rejected me before. Their actions told me I wasn't good enough. I didn't belong in their circle. Looks of disgust were on their faces. Would I experience rejection again because of this audition? Oh, how I agonized over it!

I said to myself, "They don't know I can sing. Why bother to let them know?"

I thought that settled it, but God had other plans. They held auditions after church. Most Sundays, as soon as the last Amen, Mom and I headed for the door. The only days we stayed late were the Sundays we served in the kitchen. Since this was one of those days, we were still at church.

I walked through the church and heard someone audition. She happily walked out because she'd made the team.

I congratulated her and said to myself, "I can do this."

Before I had the chance to talk myself out of it, I walked up to the people holding the audition.

Since I hadn't planned or prepared for an audition, I sang the same song the other person had sung.

The response from the leader was, "Wow, Leslie. I didn't know you could sing. Welcome to the praise team."

What? All the agonizing, fretting, worrying, and being anxious, and none of my fears had come to pass. They accepted me. Philippians 4:6-8 tells me to be anxious for nothing, but "in everything by prayer and supplication with thanksgiving make your request known to God and the peace of God which passes all understanding will guard your heart and mind."

Whoever said hindsight was 20/20 made a grand point. When I started serving in the praise team, I learned and grew. I may not have grown to the expectations of others, but I grew. As I looked back to my beginning, I saw God at work. He used the experience from the church I grew up in to set me up for success.

In the church I grew up in, I learned how to teach voice parts. First I learned soprano, then alto, and finally tenor. By the time

I left, I had taught the choir and praise team everything I knew. They had gifts and talents, and they could sing harmony without me. They still sound good to this day. I'm thankful that I had a small part to play there.

Then, as I moved to the next spot, there was the birth of the ministry of the Anointed Sisters of Praise. Now for the first time I sang. Since we had no musicians, we learned to sing with tracks. Although I learned and grew, there was more to learn.

I learned a lot from the praise team that I joined. Praise rehearsals looked different from anything I had ever known. In the church I grew up in, most rehearsals went like this. The leader picked out songs and taught parts.

Okay, sopranos repeat after me. Then the leader would do the same with the alto and tenor part. The next week they practiced the same thing until they learned the song.

Being new to the praise team meant all songs were new. There were five or six songs on the CD for the next Sunday.

Since I sang soprano, I picked out the soprano parts for all songs. I practiced in my car. I drove to and from work all week. If I had problems with the part, I let the leader know at rehearsal.

At the rehearsal, the team sang through the songs with the track. The leader listened for errors, corrected errors, and helped with trouble spots. If all went well, we needed no extra rehearsals. I learned and grew. Now I was out in front more consistently. I would do more things.

Since we were just beginning with the praise team, we had guest leaders who came in and sang. All of them wanted to know if I wanted to lead. I didn't. I enjoyed singing in the background.

One day, Darlene said, "That part sounds like you. Would you try singing this verse?"

I tried it, and she said, "That sounded good, you do these verses tomorrow and I'll sing in the background and do your part."

I was so nervous. She said I could do it, and she was right. It was a tremendous step for me, but they wanted more. Any songs that came in that range, the leaders gave me the verses.

Singing those verses was a blessing to me. Before this opportunity came, I never sang verses in front of people. I only sang verses at home or in the car with the radio, CD, or tape. I never would have tried. I never felt I could do it. Winning in this area increased my confidence. It was because of one small thing – leading verses.

In the sweet spot, growth is inevitable. In the sweet spot we grew, learned, and gained confidence. We heard things in a deeper way, in a different way than we had before. We tried new things. We found we had what it took all along.

All too often, we don't taste this sweet victory. Instead, we remain stuck in the past, stuck in familiarity, and stuck in indecision.

Will we be content to stay here or find the sweet spot? It started with making a decision that we didn't want to make. It continued in trying new things.

Will you take time to get a revelation or hindsight 2020? Will you look back on areas in which you succeeded in the past? These are clues to your sweet spot.

How did you begin in life? Where have you succeeded? We find clues to the next sweet spot in past successes and wins. Are you ready to grow? Are you willing to learn to do something different? What's one thing you can do right now? Will you continue in it?

CHAPTER

Twenty

To More Growth

In the sweet spot, some people encourage you and help you move forward. That's what the praise team did for me. I was happy and content with leading the verses.

They posed it to me as a question, "Would you like to try this verse?"

My response was, "Yes."

When I felt pushed, I responded differently. Now they wanted me to lead praise and worship, but I wasn't ready.

The leader said things like, "Everyone is a leader."

The girl who joined the praise team with me led the praise service. The other team members began leading.

Although the leader was looking at me, I wouldn't budge. I was afraid, but she couldn't see that. Also, there was not one part of me that wanted to lead praise and worship.

Although I had gotten comfortable with my singing voice, I was very insecure about my speaking voice.

People always said to me, "Speak up. I can't hear you."

Every praise team leader I'd ever seen pumped the congregation up with their words.

"Praise the Lord, everybody."

They boldly and loudly spoke to the congregation.

Don't they know? Anyone who knows me knows that I'm calm and soft-spoken. Anyone who knows me knows I am more of a one-on-one conversation type of person. Yet the push was there to lead praise and worship.

I couldn't see myself doing this. I couldn't see myself pumping up the crowd.

Even practicing alone in my car, it didn't feel like me. So I never did it. Maybe one day I'll do it. Maybe I'll never do it. At this point it's not a desire I have, so I'm comfortable not doing it. I don't feel God telling me it's time to do it. And I let peace be my umpire. Colossians 3:15

In those days when our people started leading, I had no peace. I had a lot of fear. I didn't see myself as the leader, nor did I want to be. However, the theme would not go away.

"Everyone is a leader," the leader had said, and she wouldn't let it go. I felt pushed. I didn't want to be pushed. Things felt heavy. I couldn't breathe. Every time I turned around, there was the push to lead.

Now, instead of being fearful, I became frustrated and angry. Why don't they just get off my back?

One day, out of the blue, they rocked my foundation again. The pastors told us our church was moving to a new location. I was not excited about this at all. My house was ten minutes from the church. I liked that very much.

Of course, my praise team members knew that would be an issue for me. So the next thing I heard was, "The church alive is worth the drive." And it wasn't just them. The pastors started saying it too, and one of them even tried to corner me and talk about the move. By the grace of God somebody wanted his attention, and I was able to slip out of the church and into my car.

I most definitely didn't want to drive forty minutes every Sunday and Wednesday. Don't even get me started on praise rehearsals on Monday nights, which ended at ten o'clock. In the meantime, the pressure to lead continued.

By the time the church got ready to move to the next city, I was ready for them to go.

The week of the move, I told my leader, "I am going to take a leave of absence."

On the day of the move, she let the team know of my decision. Let's just say there might have been an unpleasant scene had it not been for Elliot. Elliot had joined the praise team. He was good. He was hilarious. On that day, Elliot came to my rescue.

When someone tried to say something he would say, "But whyyyyyy?"

His face looked serious, but his voice was hysterical.

Every time he said, "But whyyyyy?" I couldn't help but laugh at him.

Thank you, Elliot, for coming to my rescue.

Looking back over it, I know my leader saw things in me I couldn't see.

One time she said, "I never led praise and worship until I came here."

She pushed me because she wanted me to have an experience, just as she had. She wanted more for me. But I wasn't ready.

I was having fun doing what I was doing, and I was okay. Maybe we are never truly ready until we want more for ourselves. I didn't want to lead, but I wanted to sing. I learned a lot during that time. I put a lot of the things I learned there into the ministry of The Anointed Sisters of Praise.

Even in the sweet spot, you must decide. You must decide how far you want to go.

Also, you must have peace in what you're doing. The things you do must come out of your heart. You can't do things because someone is pushing you to do it. You must want it for yourself. It can't be guilt or shame. It must come out of your heart.

Insecurities will always rise. In the world you will have tribulation, but be of good cheer, for I have overcome the world (John 16:33.)

I've heard someone say, "When I started something new, I was always afraid."

Insecurities will rise. As they do, it's time to have a talk with Jesus. It's time to tell Him all about your troubles. It's time to gain peace.

When insecurities rise, we're tempted to run the other way. Since we know God designed the sweet spot to push us out of our comfort zone, make sure we're not running away and hiding. We must be sure it's God's will for us. We must let the peace of God be our umpire (Colossians 3:15)

Have insecurities hindered you from reaching your full potential? Are you willing to talk to God about your insecurities? Are you willing to trust God in your situation? Are you ready to follow God, even when it makes no sense to your mind? Will you find out whether you're supposed to stay or leave?

CHAPTER

Twenty-One

To Here We Go Again

Although it made no sense to the natural mind, Mom and I were beginning again. It was time to say goodbye to church number three and hello to church number four.

We had done it in the past, but this time was different. One church after another got the thumbs down. One church had an outstanding pastor, and I took a lot of notes from his sermon.

The members were friendly and showed love, but the praise service was boring, as was the music selection. If we wanted to hear a fast song, we had to get there at the beginning because that's when they sang the only one. It was a wonderful song, but I felt I needed more.

One day, during praise and worship, I opened my eyes and looked around. I saw people smiling and lifting their hands in worship. Then I realized they loved it. I was the only one having a problem. This wasn't a good fit for me. Church four had a quick goodbye.

I was excited to try church number five, partly because it was closer to home. I checked out the praise team first and liked it. They had good harmony and a great flow. The next thing I saw were friendly people who welcomed us in. They directed us into the sanctuary.

So far this church was two for two; next was the Word. The preacher taught a good Word, but although I took notes, he was too slow for me. He talked slowly. He drifted from one side of the pulpit to the other. I just wanted him to hurry and make his point. Two out of three ain't bad but wouldn't work for me. It was time to go.

Often people talk about a ram in the bush. I believe they got this from Genesis 22. God sent Abraham into the mountains to offer his son Isaac as a sacrifice. It was a test to see if Abraham believed God, and whether he would obey Him.

Since Abraham believed God, he went to do what God instructed. He knew God had promised Isaac to him. He knew the blessings were coming through Isaac. He believed if he killed Isaac, God would raise him up.

As he held up the knife, an angel of the Lord stopped him. He showed Abraham the ram in the bush. God had provided that ram in the bush because He knew Abraham loved Him. He knew Abraham would obey Him in everything.

As the search continued for the next church, God sent our ram in the bush. One day when I got home from work Mom said she wanted to show me something interesting she'd seen in the newspaper. '

I looked at the paper and saw a guest minister from one of our former churches was starting a church in my city. Well, he was actually using space at another church's building, so his services would take place on Saturday afternoon.

This excited me because I knew it would be a good fit. I had already heard him preach on the screen. I already knew he was an excellent teacher and preacher. I already knew he would base praise service the same way.

That Saturday, Mom and I headed over there and, as expected, found the praise service to be amazing. We were disappointed to learn the leader would only be able to do it for a few more weeks because her husband was starting his own church, but then new leaders came in and they were great as well. Even my leader from a former church came. Of course she was amazing. Then another leader came.

One leader after another came to lead our praise and worship.

One day I told my mom, "We can do this. Do you want me to put our name in as volunteers for the praise service?"

She reluctantly agreed. So I put our name in the basket, but nothing happened. No one saw it. So we let it ride.

One praise service stood out to me. The praise team leader did not show up, so the pastor stepped in and did praise and worship. The reason it stood out to me was because I felt so sorry for him. Although he stepped up and did what needed to be done, I could tell he was very uncomfortable. He sang nervously, as if he were trying to remember the words. His entire body was stiff and his eyes flicked from one side to the other. Poor thing. Before that day I had never seen him be anything but confident. I could tell he had stepped out of his element.

Once again. I told Mom, "We can do this."

On the next Saturday I asked the pastor, "Did you get our card?"

"What card?" he asked.

When I explained about the note I'd left about me and Mom leading praise and worship, he got excited.

"Sure! You guys can lead praise and worship!"

He canceled the other praise and worship leaders and we began. Now, we had led praise and worship in the past, but until now we had never done so consistently. This was an entirely new thing. And, as always, God's Presence showed up. Another new development occurred while we were going to this church: my dad came with us.

All my life, church had been something Mom and I did together. I don't know why he had decided to attend, but it was nice. He enjoyed service. He cleaned, took out the trash, moved tables and chairs neatly in place. When we started singing, he helped us up and down the stairs.

Three or four small steps took us on stage. Mom gave the intro, and we sang. We sang two fast, upbeat songs and one slow song.

At the end of praise and worship, we sang little melodies to God. "We worship You, Lord. We love You Lord. Hallelujah."

Then my dad helped us off the stage and moved the microphone and the stands to a far corner of the stage.

As we sang these simple melodies, the congregation joined us. The presence of God filled the room. People stood and raised their hands. Some even cried. The presence of God shifted the atmosphere. It prepared the way for the Word of God to be ministered freely. All was well.

Sometimes opportunities came to us, but we didn't take them. It was a place for us, but we wouldn't step out. It was because of a low-level fear. *Can I do this? Can I succeed?*

You never know unless you try. For me, it was doing praise and worship service. What is it for you? What have you been putting off? If you saw someone struggling and could help, would you? Are you ready and willing to step out and try? Are you ready to walk by faith (2 Corinthians 5:7)? You can do it.

God gave you everything you need. God builds on something we've already used.

Mom and I had been praising Him for years. He then built on that by allowing us to do praise and worship consistently. He knew we needed practice.

What has God given you? Are you willing to take time to write down what you're good at? What gifts, skills, talents, and abilities do you have? What have you done with those things in the past?

Maybe God wants to build on those gifts, skills, talents, and abilities. Is He trying to get you to the next level? Will you use what you have to help others? Since you never know how long a season will last, will you jump in so you don't miss your opportunity?

I'm reminded of a lame man by a pool. When the angel stirred the pool, it made completely well the first one who entered. For thirty-eight years this lame man was at the pool, but he never got in. He missed many opportunities. He made many excuses. He made many mistakes.

One day Jesus came to him. Jesus asked, "Do you want to be well?" Do you want to be whole? Do you want your sweet spot? Then take up your mat and walk. Jesus was saying, "Do something." (John 5:1-15)

Now I am asking you, do you want to find your sweet spot? Are you ready? What's one thing you can do this week?

The pool is stirring. With Jesus, you don't have to be the first one in. You can stop making excuses. You can take up your bed and walk. You can win.

CHAPTER

Twenty-Two

To You've Got to Be Kidding Me

You know what happened, don't you? I'm sure by now you can just about guess.

My family and I enjoyed church. We had a place all of us belonged. Although the church was small, we called forth members from the North, South, East, and West. I fully expected members to show up. All was well, or so I thought.

During one of our prayer times before church, the pastor made an announcement. At the end of that month we would merge with the church that owned the building.

You've got to be kidding me! I thought, *Not again!*

To me, this seemed like it had come out of the blue. By this point, I was beyond frustrated and even a little angry. Why did this keep happening to me?

I liked the church I was attending, and I didn't want to go some-where else. If I had wanted to go to the other church I would have. Now we were merging together, and I didn't think it was a good thing. How can two separate things merge together as one? How could one church have two pastors? What would praise service be like? What did the other pastor sound like? Was he as good as the one I had? Although I had doubts, I went.

Although disappointed, I went to the first service. It was official. They had merged us together. Although our pastor preached, we did not sing.

"You can stand or sit," the other pastor said, "Do whatever you want to do."

What? We were about inviting the congregation to join in. Stand on your feet. No matter how much we liked our Saturday pastor, we knew this was not going to work for us.

One reason the other pastor may have wanted to merge was because of our praise team. The praise team from the other pastor sang, but they were nothing like us. They didn't have the energy we brought. It was not exciting. People in the congregation barely paid attention to them. I wondered, would they even like us and our way?

One reason *our* pastor wanted to merge was because our church membership was so small, much smaller than the other congrega-tion. Now, when we sat in our regular seats we spoke to others, but that was it. The rest of the time I felt alone. When it came time to discuss something with the members in our area, I only talked to Mom. I didn't feel like I belonged.

The church now had two leaders, with two pastors. That made no sense to me. It made no sense to my dad either. He stopped coming. Mom and I went for a few more weeks, but we knew our days there were numbered. Even when they finally got around to asking us to lead praise and worship, we declined. What was the point, when we knew we were not staying?

Once again, we left the church with nowhere else to go. Though I wasn't happy about this. I'd rather be in no place than the wrong place. Once again, my family and I visited churches. Mom and I revisited some churches we had already been to.

One place we revisited had had an overhaul. The congregation wasn't mixed as much as before. Before it had been a half-and-half mixture. When we went before, the congregation was a beautiful mixture of black and white. When we came back most of the black people were gone. It was basically a white congregation with a few black people here and there. It shocked me. Now there were different praise team leaders. I think the former leaders mixed songs so different people would come. Things had changed. That church had changed. I had changed. When change takes place, there is no going back. There can only be a moving forward.

So again and again we tried and tried. We searched and searched, but no place seemed to be for us.

We found something closer to our house. The people welcomed us, but it wasn't for us. After church I came home, sighed heavily, laid down, and went to sleep. By this time I was getting weary of all this searching. If I was going to feel like this after every service, if I wasn't getting my needs met, there was no need to go to church at all.

Finally, Mom and I turned on the computer, pulled up our chairs, got out some pens and paper, and watched church on the Internet. We had exhausted all other possibilities.

Once I heard an evangelist say, "You've got to come to the end of yourself."

At the time I didn't know what she meant. Now I did, because I felt like I was living it. There was no place to go. No place to try. No place to belong. It was the end.

It was also the beginning.

Matthew 6:33 says, "Seek ye first the kingdom of God and all these things will be added unto you."

Now was not the time to seek another church. It was time to seek God. It was time to seek His way of being and doing right. Not my will, but His will be done.

In life, we're all searching for the sweet spot. We're searching for the place where we belong. We can tell when something was the wrong spot or the right spot. Often we give up prematurely. Sometimes we made a practice of giving up again and again.

Along the way, life throws twists and turns. Although disappointments may come again and again, we can still win. In the world, you will have tribulation, but be of good cheer, for I have overcome the world John 16:33.

Life is constantly presenting us with choices, circumstances in which we must decide. We want to get in bed, pull the covers over our heads, and wish things would stay the same. This brings to mind another of my favorite shows, *Sister, Sister,* when Tamera tried to do this because she didn't want to go to college.

Tamera discovered that people who made impressive accomplishments in this world were afraid. They wanted to stay on the sidelines, too. They wanted things to stay the same.

The decision is ours to make. Are you tired of settling in the wrong spot? Tired of going around the same mountain over and over again? Isn't it about time you find the sweet spot where we can flow despite challenges?

Knowing there is a sweet spot, even when you can't see it, requires faith. What can you do to stir up your faith? Why not try asking God for your sweet spot? Why not surrender to His will instead of pursuing your own?

PART 3

✦

FINALLY

CHAPTER

Twenty-Three

To Being Fully Committed

One thing I enjoyed in the church I grew up in was songs like "Fully Committed." We need to be fully committed.

Although the journey to find the church had been full of major disappointments, commitment was there. Even through discouragement I kept going, kept searching, kept trying, kept asking.

Matthew 7:7, "Ask and it shall be given." No matter what I saw, I knew God had a place for me. Sometimes up, sometimes down, but Jesus had a place for me. I just knew it.

That "knowing" was faith. The just shall live by faith (Romans 1:17). That's how God designed us to fulfill His will for our lives. If we walk by sight, the circumstances we see can cause us to give up, cave in, and quit. Let us not be weary in well doing for in due season, we will reap if we faint not (Galatians 6:9).

Often we get weary based on what we've seen. It doesn't look like what we're doing is working, so we quit. It's time to break this vicious cycle of quitting based on our circumstances.

How do we break this cycle? We change our focus. Now it's time to look to Jesus, the Author and Finisher of our faith (Hebrews 12:2).

Although He was facing the cross, the beating, and the humiliation, He had joy. Even in the most trying times, He prayed to His Father in the Garden of Gethsemane. He ended His prayer with, "Not my will, but Yours be done (Luke 22:42). He knew His Resurrection would benefit many. He knew what He was going through was worth it. He knew *we* were worth it. Jesus committed Himself.

Are you ready to change your focus? How often do your situations discourage you? Where can you fully commit, as Jesus did? Are you willing to push past hurt, disappointment, and discouragement?

Knowing God has a plan for your life releases faith. It can cause you to believe despite what you see. All things are possible to them that believe (Mark 9:23). Believing allows you to push through rather than give up on your sweet spot.

CHAPTER

Twenty-Four

❧

To Turning North

What's the use? Repeatedly, I kept getting shut down. Repeatedly, something happened that pulled the rug out from under me. Christ is the solid rock on which I stand. All other ground is sinking sand. All other ground is sinking sand.

What am I doing wrong? Why does this keep happening to me? Where am I supposed to be? Is something wrong with me? I don't see many people going through this church thing. Then again, maybe they have another mountain they keep circling around.

One day, God reminded me of one of my aunt's first sermons. She talked about how the Israelites had wandered in the wilderness.

She came down from the pulpit to the floor. There was someone who had a big sign with the letter A on it. As she preached, she kept going around the person with the sign. She went around and around, over and over again, to show the congregation a picture. She let us know that we are on a journey, but sometimes one thing trips us up. Instead of moving forward, we just keep circling it. We just go around and around the same mountain, never defeating it or moving forward. We are stuck.

Then she stopped. She stopped to let us know that God can get our attention. Even in going around the same mountain, trial, situation, circumstance, et cetera… God can speak a Word to us.

God said, "You have made your way around this mountain long enough; Now turn North." (Deuteronomy 2:2)

That part of the message spoke to me. It meant something different. You've been here long enough. You've been sick and tired long enough. Frustrated and disappointed long enough. You've been depressed and rejected long enough. Quit going around the same mountain repeatedly. Turn North.

North is upward. North looks past the circumstances. North looks to the hills from which comes your help. So there I was sitting in front of the computer screen with some notebook paper. I was looking to see what God would say to me. I decided not to go here and there anymore. I turned North.

The temptation to give up is very real when we're discouraged and frustrated, When we've been in a continual state where things are not working, we feel like quitting. What's the use?

God doesn't waste any of our experiences. As we stop looking at ourselves and start looking to Him, He will give us a lifeline. He will give a word, an idea, a thought, that challenges and encourages us to turn North.

When I was tired and felt like giving up, God gave me a Word. The Bible is His Word. I realized it had helped me. I realized I needed to know what God said about my situation.

All you need is one Word from God to turn the entire situation around. Now we have Siri and Google. You no longer have to look up scriptures from a big concordance. Now you can just ask or type and click.

Have you felt like giving up lately? Are you tired of doing the same thing repeatedly without seeing results? Are you ready to stop the insanity?

What do you need? Is it peace? Are you willing to ask Siri to help you find scriptures of peace? Do you need healing? Will you type it in Google? Will you find the scriptures that cover your situation? Will you read and meditate on those scriptures several times a day?

What's one thing you can do this week that shows you're ready to turn North?

CHAPTER

Twenty-Five

To What God Says in Scripture

What did the scriptures have to say about my church? Hebrews 10:25: "Not forsaking the assembly of ourselves together, as the manner of some is, but exhorting one another: so much the more as you see the day approaching."

What did that mean to me? It meant I was not about to forsake going to church. Others did, and they still do. They don't go because someone hurt them too badly. They had trusted too much. They couldn't bring themselves to go again.

Although I understood their hurt, I knew my place was still in church, that there was a place for me to belong. I too had experienced shame, hurt, and disappointment, but I believed Hebrews 10:25 was true for me. I was to share this journey with other believers. I was to exhort or encourage them. They were to encourage me.

I wanted and needed a church that taught me the Word.

According to Matthew 16:18, Jesus said to Peter, "Upon this rock, I will build My church…"

That's what I wanted and needed.

"… the gates of hell shall not prevail against it."

Everywhere I had gone before, the gates of hell seemed to have prevailed. Yet I still looked to see what God said. I had faith. I believed God.

"Without faith it is impossible to please God, for he who comes to God must believe that He is and that He is a rewarder of them that diligently seek Him (Hebrews 11:6)."

I believed it. Though it wasn't yet available in a way my five physical senses could perceive it, I believed. I had faith that there was a place for me.

In scripture, Jesus found a man lying by a pool. When angels stirred the water, the first person who got into the pool was healed of all his infirmity. Jesus saw the man who had been in that same spot for thirty-eight years.

Jesus asked him, "Do you want to be whole?"

The sick man answered Him, "Sir, I have no man to put me into the pool when the water is stirred up, but while I am coming, another steps down before me." (John 5:7)

The man came to Jesus with his excuses. It was like he was saying the only reason he had been there so long was because of others.

Today, Jesus is still asking us, "Do you want to be whole?" Do you want to be healed? Do you want that promotion? If so, how long will you continue hanging around the pool?

When will you jump in and get wet? When will you figure out what you want? Will you stay stuck by the pool with your excuses? Will you blame other people for your condition? When will you seek God and see what His Word has to say about your situation? Will you allow past hurts to continue to keep you stuck in the same spot?

Will you press forward? Will you believe God? Will you let your faith grow? What can you do to keep the momentum going?

CHAPTER

Twenty-Six

To What God Says: Confessions

Are you tired of experiencing the same problems repeatedly? Are you ready for some kind of change? Do you want to experience a brighter future above where you are today? Then it is time to watch your mouth – to watch your confessions.

Our confessions are important, and the Bible has a lot to say about our words.

Psalms 19:14 instructs, "Let the words of my mouth and the meditation of my heart be acceptable in Your sight. Oh, Lord my strength and my redeemer."

Proverbs 18:21 allows us to see that "Death and life are in the power of the tongue. "

It reminded me of that ridiculous thing we said as kids: "Sticks and stones may break my bones, but words will never hurt."

Death is in the power of the tongue. Words are powerful. Life is in the power of the tongue.

In the beginning, in Genesis I, God saw what we would call a "hot mess." The earth was dark, void, and empty. It looked hopeless. It looked impossible. It looked beyond repair.

Despite all that, God said, "Let there be light," and there was light.

He continued to speak. He saw what He spoke.

Genesis 1:26 says He made us in His image and after His likeness. I knew I could do the same thing. I had Hebrews 10:25, Matthew 16:18, and Hebrews 11:6 to guide me. I wrote what I wanted.

What did I want? I wanted a church where the pastor taught the Word of God in a way I could understand it. I wanted a praise team that sang in harmony. I wanted a place where I was accepted as I was. I wrote it down on paper so I could see it. I wanted to keep it before my eyes. Then I confessed what I wanted along with these scriptures. I spoke them out loud. I knew faith comes by hearing. I got in agreement with God. "Can two walk together except they be agreed (Amos 3:3)?"

Although there were no physical changes in the circumstances, there was a change. When I looked at my situation, I no longer felt hopeless. When I looked at my situation, I no longer felt it was unsolvable or beyond repair. Now I had hope. As they sang in the Baptist Church, I had a feeling everything's gonna be alright.

I stopped the back-and-forth and from here to there. I concentrated on agreement with God. I kept praying; I kept confessing the Word. And when I got tired or frustrated, I turned to Galatians 6:9: "Let us not be weary in well doing for if we faint not we will receive our reward."

I said, "God, Your Word says, not to forsake the assembling of yourselves. Show me where to go so I can walk in line with Your Word."

Like a dog with a bone, I refused to let go.

We only move as we're ready for some kind of change. One of the smallest and biggest changes we can make is paying attention to the words of our mouths.

Are you ready to change your words for the better? Are you ready to get in agreement with God? Will you find at least three scriptures concerning your situation? Will you keep those scriptures and confessions going until you see the desired results? Will you listen to yourself? What is one thing you have said repeatedly that has you stuck now? How can you improve the situation? It's time to speak in line with something higher than what you are speaking now (Psalms 19:14).

CHAPTER

Twenty-Seven

To What God Says: The Vision

Are you living the same way over and over again and expecting different results? Are you tired of the insanity? If so, as Habakkuk 2:2 says, "Write the vision."

There I was, sitting in front of my computer, listening to the preacher on screen; I was learning and taking notes.

Where did I want to be? I wanted to be in my church with actual people. I knew being in a particular place was God's will for me. So I wrote the vision. I used the scriptures. I used the confessions.

I had been here before with the ministry of The Anointed Sisters of Praise. We had sat on that big grey Greyhound bus talking about where we wanted to be. We talked about what our ministry was to be about.

I remember it like it was yesterday.

"What should our ministry be about?" I'd asked.

Mom responded, "Singing with the anointing."

"I like praise and worship," my cousin added, "so that's the style."

My cousin chimed in, "It's not to be just a singing ministry. We've got to use God's Word."

I don't know how I got roped into teaching, but it fell on me. I needed that experience. It helped me dive deeper into the sweet spot.

We didn't just talk about our vision for The Anointed Sisters of Praise; we also wrote it down. And it had come to pass. Now, that was where I was with my church. I wrote the vision. I read it. I confessed it. So it didn't matter that I seemed stuck at home in front of a computer screen. I knew there was a way out. I believed it despite what I saw.

Too often we've been stuck in familiarity and in the same spot. We saw no way out. Having a vision is a way out.

We've been guilty of life as usual, even though we didn't like it. Insanity is doing the same thing over and over again, expecting to see different results. When we are ready for different results, we must do something different. We must decide what we want and write the vision.

Are you ready to break out? Will you take some time to write your vision and make it plain? Start from where you are now and where you want to be? Make it so big that you know you can't do it without God's divine guidance.

Will you take time out to write the vision? What do you want for your family, social life, health and wellness, spiritual life, work, business, finances, et cetera? Where are you now? Write it down. Where do you want to be? Write it down.

CHAPTER

Twenty-Eight

To Preparation

Though we had no church home, the ministry of The Anointed Sister of Praise kept going. We had no engagements. We had no prospects. Yet we kept practicing and crafting our songs. We kept experiencing God's presence, even during rehearsals.

Some might have asked, "Why do you keep doing what you're doing? Why don't you just stop? What good is it doing you?"

It reminded me of Job and his wife. He had lost everything. His children were dead. His cattle died.

"Why don't you curse God and die," she said (Job 2:9). She was telling him that trusting God was not working for him. He'd been a good person, but all these things were happening, so what was the use? Why not just get this thing over with?

Things turned from bad to worse for Job. His friends said, "This happened to you because you've done wrong. Confess your sin."

But that wasn't necessarily the case. You see, in Job 1 and 2, we saw satan coming after Job. First, he watched Job. Then, satan thought Job would curse God if he lost all his stuff. Finally, satan tried to prove to God that Job wouldn't trust Him if he lost it all.

What if he is doing the same thing to us today? Have you ever felt like when it rains, it pours? If it ain't one thing, it's another. That's probably how Job felt too. Yet through it all, he never once cursed God. No matter how much he was tested and tempted, Job never gave up. In the end, he got a double portion of everything he had lost.

Though I too felt like giving up many times, I kept standing. One day, I came home to find a message from one of our supporters on the answering machine. She'd had a meeting planned for months and now, at the last minute, she found out the praise team wouldn't be there. She was in a bind and wanted to know if we could fill in.

This person had always been good to us. No matter what, she chose us for her big events. Although I never did anything last minute, she was our friend and she needed help.

I had peace about telling her we would lead the praise service. In two days, we found the right songs and practiced before the big day. I looked through several sets. None of these felt right. As I continued searching, I prayed.

"Lord, help me find the right set. You know who will be there. You know what they need."

Then I found not one set but two. "Thank You, Jesus."

Since I had no time to figure it out, I trusted God. And since we had continued to practice regularly whether we had an engagement or not, things worked out really well, really fast. We breathed a sigh of relief when we realized one set felt right. Now we were prepared for the meeting at church.

Just because some things didn't work for us, it doesn't mean we can't help others out. Just because we feel like giving up doesn't mean we have to. We're to do unto others as we would have them do unto us.

No matter what you're going through, you have something you're good at that can help someone else. What is it? How can you use it? Who can you help? You may just find out that helping them will help you as well.

Sometimes helping people may seem inconvenient for you. Will you help anyway? God blessed you to be a blessing. Find the balance and do what is right for you. Ask. Seek. Knock. (Matthew 7:7)

It is not possible to help everyone, but you can seek God for who you are to help. Just by helping someone, you may gain strength to keep moving forward and not give up. Your reward could be right on the other side.

CHAPTER

Twenty-Nine

To The Meeting

I prepared The Anointed Sisters of Praise for the meeting. We walked into the familiar sanctuary, clothed in a dark purple and a light lavender. Even the steps leading to the pulpit where we would sing were covered in light lavender. The cushioned lavender chairs were soft and cozy. The carpet was purple, which complemented things nicely. It was nice. It was homey.

It was time for us to lead praise and worship. After someone prayed, another person introduced us. We walked up the lavender stairs to the pulpit area. A deacon helped us up the stairs so we wouldn't fall. What a gentleman!

As we stood behind the microphones, Mom exhorted the people.

She said, "Clap your hands all ye people, shout unto God with a voice of triumph (Psalm 47:1)."

The congregations stood up, clapped, and shouted.

As I nodded towards my dad, he hit the play button and started playing the CD track we had chosen. We ministered to the Lord.

I still remember the set we sang: "Shout"; "We Have Overcome"; and "When I Think About the Lord."

During those three songs, God set the atmosphere into peaceful, still, and calm. It was an energized atmosphere. After we ministered, the congregation was ready to receive the Word.

The man who preached was ready. He did an excellent job. The occasion for the program was a pastor appreciation program. The guest minister turned to scriptures like Ephesians 4:11-16.

He showed us through this Word that the pastor was a gift. God gave him to the people. Because of the pastor's teaching and praying, the people received tools to be built up. Because of the pastor, the people could grow up in Christ and be a blessing to others.

The guest minister continued his sermon and exhorted the people.

"Since the pastor is a gift from God to you, cover him in prayer. As he teaches you, do the Word."

When he finished preaching, he prayed over the congregation and the pastor.

That service blessed me. It never would have happened if we hadn't agreed to help somebody in their time of need.

Everyone is so busy. We feel so busy that we don't have time to help others. If it doesn't fit into our schedule, we don't do it. We often do what we want to. We don't do what we don't want to do.

God wants us to help people. Can you help? Who have you helped before? Helping others causes blessings in our lives. If you are ready to be blessed, help somebody.

After service, I spotted the guest minister across the room.

I looked at Mom and said, "Let's go over there and tell him what a good job he did."

Mom agreed. "Okay. Yes, he did a good job."

So we made our way to him.

Normally we would have stayed on the other side of the room we were in. Or we would have already left to go home. But that day we were still there, so boldly we went to talk to a guest minister we didn't even know.

When we got to him, we had an interesting conversation.

I said to him, "We really enjoyed your message."

He replied, "I really enjoyed your ministry. You ushered in the presence of God, which allowed me to teach."

We were overjoyed to hear that. "Wow! Thank you."

"Thank *you,*" he replied.

It was the next part of our conversation that I will never forget. He gave us his church business card with his website on it.

He said, "If you go to this site you can see our services online."

I grasped the card and thanked him. How ironic. He didn't know I was already sitting at home watching service on the Internet. It was like confirmation that I had been doing the right thing at the time.

As Mom and I reached out to help someone else, God blessed us. God set the atmosphere for the Word by us. The message of the guest pastor blessed us. The conversation after the service blessed us.

What are you waiting for? Do you want to be blessed? Then help someone else. You reap what you sow (Galatians 6:7). What good things can you sow?

CHAPTER

Thirty

To It's Not Too Late

Although I kept the card, it was a few months before I did anything with it. When you're stuck a long time, it's easy to just stay where we are. It's easy to procrastinate. It's easy to say, I'll do that later. In most cases, later never comes.

In my case, "later" came and I acted on it.

One Sunday, as I held the card in my hand I asked Mom, "Do you want to watch that pastor we heard before?"

"Okay," she said, already pulling up her chair. We watched the church service from the comfort of our own home.

The first test of a church for me was the praise service. The praise leader sang with a track, just like we did.

Unlike us, she sang with the track that had background vocals on it. She sang the verses and led the worship. She sang songs we knew. We liked her. The first test of this church passed for us.

The next step of a church for me was the teaching of the Word. Since the pastor didn't preach, we watched again.

The next time we looked at the service on the Internet, the pastor led the praise service, but he still didn't preach.

After watching off and on for several weeks Mom, Dad and I decided to go in person. Thank God for Google. The church wasn't in our city, but all I had to do was plug in the address, and mine, and within seconds a map appeared.

On the way there, we chatted about what we might experience.

"If this pastor did that well in another person's pulpit," I said, "think of what it might look like to hear him in his own house."

We almost didn't make it. We almost gave up. Google couldn't help us understand all the crooks and turns. We couldn't find it. We couldn't figure out which way to go.

My dad saw a gentleman sitting on his porch. He stopped and asked for directions. My dad explained he was with his wife and daughter and was trying to find a church in the nearby area. The man got on his computer and tried to Google from where we were.

As Mom and I continued to sit in the car, the man's wife came out to us. She was so friendly.

She said, "You don't have to stay in the car. Come onto the porch."

Then she showed us her flowers. Since Mom loved flowers, she enjoyed visiting with this woman we didn't even know. The woman even cut off some flowers for Mom to take home and plant.

With a big smile on her face she said, "Stop by anytime."

After my dad got better directions we were off again. The couple left on the way to their church. On the way down the road, Dad saw the sign. We had passed it, but now all we had to do was turn around.

That sweet couple, who was behind us, also saw the sign. They flagged us down then pulled off to the side of the road. Dad turned around and pulled off to the other side, then walked across the street and thanked them once again. What a blessing they were to us that day – not once, but twice!

The problem was, getting lost had made us extremely late for the service. Although we found the church, we were too embarrassed to go in.

"Let's come back next week now that we know where it is," I suggested.

My mom said, "That sounds good to me."

My dad said, "I'm going in."

So we hesitantly followed.

As we moved closer to the door, I heard a woman preaching. Slowly, we turned the handle and went in. We sat down quickly in the first seats we saw.

It was a sanctuary that had a stage upfront. There were folding chairs neatly lined up on both sides of the church.

A camera section separated the back rows. The cameras looked like the ones from the movie sets in Hollywood. Of course it made sense since cameras had to be there. Those cameras made it possible for us to see the program on the internet.

Then I turned my attention to the woman on the stage giving a Mother's Day message. I took out my white folder with the three prongs. Then I gently pulled out a piece of college-ruled notebook paper. I wanted to take notes because the message sounded good.

Since it was Mother's Day, they gave her the opportunity to speak. She spoke from what she knew. I could tell it was from her personal relationship with God. As she spoke, I felt it. I wanted more of what she had.

After she spoke, the pastor got up. He spoke to the congregation; he thanked the visitors for coming. Then he thanked us for coming.

Although it had been several months, he still remembered who we were. He remembered the name he heard and called us by name. Wow! Once again, he had impressed me.

Procrastination almost caused me to miss out on a wonderful experience. Although I had the card, I kept putting off going onto the website or to the church.

Many times we miss out on things. We think we'll do it later, but later never comes.

What things have you been putting off lately? Are you willing to make a list of them? Will you set some goals and deadlines for yourself? It's time to stop missing God's best because of procrastination.

On our journey to finding the place, many obstacles may rise. We may have gotten lost. We may have felt we would never find the right path. Maybe we procrastinated and did not investigate the possibility of something different. We have not prepared for something different. We've been miserable and stuck.

Do you want to see something different? Are you willing to investigate and see the possibilities? Will you write them down and decide on something different? What's one thing you can do to prepare for it?

When I stopped procrastinating and started preparing for something different, things happened for my good. (Romans 8:28) What good things can happen for you? The possibilities are unlimited.

I thought it was too late to go into the church. Often we think it's too late to do something. We think, "I'm too old." Since we think it's too late, we don't bother to go in. We fail to open the door and walk in to receive what God has prepared for us.

What if I told you it's not too late? It can still happen to you and for you. If God is for you, who can be against you (Romans 8:31)? God is for you. You can receive what God has for you. He has thoughts to prosper you and give you an expected end (Jeremiah 29:11).

Where have you been thinking it's too late? As long as you have breath, it is not too late. Since you won't always have breath, what are you willing to do? What is one door you can open today that will get you closer to your sweet spot?

CHAPTER

Thirty-One

To the Invite

After service the pastor came to talk to us. He asked, "Would you like to sing praise and worship next week? I have an opening."

It shocked Mom and me. The last time we had sung at church it had been a last-minute request, and at a church we had been to many times.

I was thinking, *Who does that? Who asks someone who had never been to the church before to sing? Nobody!*

We didn't have time to go home and pray about it for five weeks. He wanted an answer, so I said we would do it.

At the same time, I wondered what I was getting myself into. He had heard us, but the congregation had not. What if they didn't like our style? Pushing all questions aside, I started to prepare mentally for the next week.

My mental preparation began with God. I sought Him on the songs. I shared my nervousness and excitement.

"Lord, I don't understand what is going on. Part of me wants to run. Part of me wants to run on and see what will happen. I trust You."

I turned my apprehension around. I turned the negative into a positive.

In my mind I had thought, "What if they don't like us? What if we mess up?"

Then I thought of something else. What if they like us? What if they receive us? What if we just did our part and let God do His?"

Of course, in addition to the mental preparation there was also physical preparation. I picked out the songs and we rehearsed diligently throughout the week.

On the next Sunday, we went back to the church. This time they invited us. We arrived early to check the microphones and the music volume.

"Can Mom's microphone be a little louder than mine?" I asked the pastor, who also ran the equipment.

We did another playback until all seemed right with the sound.

We were a little nervous, but we didn't stop. The music came naturally; I knew what I wanted. I knew how to get the sound I needed. There was no fear. We did what we always had done. God's presence showed up, as always.

Next week came, and we ministered for the first time to a new congregation. They received us. Afterwards, the congregation came up and thanked us. They enjoyed praise and worship.

Without missing a beat, the pastor asked again, "I have someone next week, would you like to sing again in two weeks?

Once again I said yes without hesitation. In fact, I looked forward to seeing the person who led praise and worship in person. Up to that point we had only seen her on the Internet.

When you are secure in who you are and in what you do, all is well. Another praise leader did not intimidate us. In fact, we welcomed the chance to hear from her. She was one reason we visited. As we knew we would, we enjoyed her ministry.

Through her we found out that the church had been praying for a praise and worship leader. They were praying for us to come. No one prayed harder than she did because she was ready to step down.

Later, when she stepped down, she continued to encourage us. She was secure in what she did, too. Thank you, April.

An invitation is a request for someone to go somewhere or to do something. They gave an invitation. We accepted.

We've often received invitations and turned them down. We thought things like it's too late, or it's too short notice. We can't do it because... Excuses, excuses. What are we afraid of? Why won't we accept the invitations extended to us for different things?

How long will you go around the same mountain? How many times have you made excuses? What has been coming to your mind lately of something you need to do?

I believe that is your invitation. Revelation 3:20 "Behold, I stand at the door and knock if any man hears My voice, open the door, I will come in to him, and will sup with him, and he with Me."

For me, accepting that invitation was a success that led to more invitations. So what's it going to be? We've missed out so many times. We've missed out on so much by not accepting the invitations we've received. We made excuses and stayed in the same place. Deep down inside, we knew we were ready for more.

What are you good at? When you're good at something, you do it with ease. God has gifted you with it. What comes naturally to you? God gave it to you to use and help others. How have you used your gifts in the past? God wants you to use them now.

What do people ask you to do? Where are your invitations coming from? Are you willing to accept them?

There is a voice inside you that wants to keep you safe. It also keeps you in safe places. You have no adventure. You just exist.

Are you just existing? Do you want to make a difference in this world? You can do it. Accept it. Believe it. Receive it. Yes, I can. Yes, you can.

CHAPTER

Thirty-Two

To What's Going Out

Earlier I mentioned that you know when you've reached the sweet spot. Things start coming out of you that you never knew were in you. Things you knew were there started coming out in a greater way.

A year after the invitation to sing, we joined that church. How did we know it was the sweet spot? Double anointing. When we came to the church, God had anointed us. God doubled that anointing. In every praise and worship service we did, God's presence showed up mightily. Our confidence had risen. Our voices got stronger. Our ministry had arrived.

In first Kings 19:19, Elisha was plowing. Elijah invited Elisha to go with him. He followed Elijah and became his servant. He watched as Elijah performed miracle after miracle. Elijah raised the dead. He called fire from heaven (1 Kings 18:41- 45).

At the time God took Elijah away, Elisha asked for a double portion of the anointing Elijah had. This is how we know he received it. Elijah, his predecessor, performed eight miracles. Elisha performed 16. He purified contaminated water (2 Kings 2), multiplied the widow's oil (2 Kings 4), raised the dead, and so on.

I say The Anointed Sisters of Praise reached the double anointing. Jesus died for us to receive the anointing. Then we got into the sweet spot under our pastor and his anointing. As a result more burdens were removed and more yokes destroyed. More power of God was experienced. More of the Presence of God was experienced.

Something we did before started coming out in a greater measure. God wants that for all of us. He came that we may have life and have it more abundantly (John 10:10). Often we settle for less than the best. It's not too late for us.

It is not too late for you. You've got what it takes because God put it in you. He's given you all things that pertain to life and godliness (2 Peter 1:3). As we talk to Him about our lives and get to know Him, what was hidden will be brought to light. It will be revealed. (Mark 4:22) It will be like fire shut up in your bones (Jeremiah 20:9). It will come out.

Examine yourself to see what gifts, talents, skills, and abilities you have. What situation have you used those things in the past? How are you using them now? If you're in the beginning stages, it may come out as a trickle. As you grow, it grows. In the wrong spot they can't grow fully. In the sweet spot you can expect to receive double. Are you ready?

Motivation Meditation with Leslie V

Back in school, English was one of my favorite subjects, partly because I'd always loved to read. It was a definite "A." As an adult, I was often asked by others about proper grammar. One coworker called me her "English teacher" because I made sure her letters or emails to supervisors or other agencies were correct. Even at home, Mom would ask me questions about English. She also called me her "English Teacher."

But though I loved English, I had never done much writing. Then one day, I just sat down and began to write. I read the things I had written to Mom.

"That sounds good," she said, "Wow! That came from you."

I continued writing and sharing with my mom. I then decided that if I wrote consistently for three months I would share it with my pastor. I gave myself this challenge because I knew I had a habit of starting things and not completing them.

Three months later, I approached my pastor for his feedback on my writings. He listened quietly until I was finished reading, then he said, "Sounds like a podcast to me."

I asked, "What's that?"

He showed me some examples on his phone. We listened to portions of some podcasts. I heard their messages and saw that I could take my writings and record them.

I began my podcast, Motivation Meditation with Leslie V, in November 2018. Though this was definitely way out of my comfort zone, I loved it. I loved the fact that I could make a difference to someone. That first episode got eighty-eight plays. I was so excited! There I was, an unknown person, yet people were listening to me.

Today, the podcast is flourishing. It's a devotional style study that gives tools to live the best life ever, overcome weaknesses, grow in a deeper personal relationship with God, and fulfill their God-given destiny. You can check it out on Apple iTunes, Google play, Spotify, Stitcher, Castbox, or you can pull it up on kingdomrock. org/mmlv.

Oftentimes, we don't take the time to see what's coming out of our lives. Is it something bad, or something good? "A good tree cannot bring forth evil fruit, neither can a corrupt tree bring forth good fruit. Wherefore by their fruits you shall know them (Matthew 7:16-20)."

Where are you? What are you producing, and how much? Where do your gifts shine through? If your answers are full of uncertainty, it's time to take a deeper look. Are you at a new beginning where only a trickle flows? Have you been in the same spot, producing nothing new, no fruit of significance? How can you change? What can you change? Where is the sweet spot for you?

CHAPTER

Thirty-Three

❧

To the Future

In the sweet spot, I'm not stuck. I look forward to the future. When I look to the future, I'm not filled with dread, but with hope. Faith is the substance of things hoped for (Hebrews 11:1).

What am I hoping for? Writing songs and having CDs for The Anointed Sisters of Praise. I look forward to having engagements all over. I look forward to singing all our own, original songs.

I'm also looking forward to speaking engagements from this book. I'm excited about creating online courses and teaching groups. I have gifts of encouragement and teaching, and I want to use them to the fullest.

In the sweet spot, the possibilities are unlimited. All things are possible to him that believes. (Mark 9:23).

When I began my writing class, I wrote out a vision. The closer I got to finishing the book, the vision began speaking.

It was saying, "This is possible." All things are possible to him that believes, and I trust in Him.

What if? What if I had not moved out of the longing for something new? What if I had never moved out of my comfort zone? What if I had never moved when new twists and turns arose? What would have happened had I not pushed through rejection and being ignored?

What would've happened had I said, "No, it's too short notice, I can't sing? What would have happened had I not said yes to the invitation to lead the praise and worship? What if I had given up? What if I hid my gifts? I wouldn't be standing in this sweet spot or looking for more to come in the future.

Sometimes we look to the future with dread, doubt, and frustration. We do that because we're stuck in indecision and the comfort of familiarity. We couldn't move forward because we're too busy hanging out in the past.

In Genesis God spoke to Terah, Abraham's father. God told him to go to a certain place. On his journey to that place, he entered Haran and settled there, instead of continuing to the place God had told him to go. The next thing we hear is that Terah died in Haran.

Would you want to die without making the impact God wanted you to have?

On my journey to find my sweet spot, there were many disappointments. There were many opportunities to give up. In the end, I was exactly where I was supposed to be. Remember, God is no respecter of persons; He created a sweet spot for everyone.

We can find it and walk in it. What are you waiting for? It's time to turn North.

Ephesians 2:10 said, "You were God's workmanship, created in Christ Jesus for good works.

Will you keep moving so you can make the impact in this world God created you to make? Let us not be weary in well doing, for we shall reap if we faint not (Galatians 6:9).

My journey started at the church where I was born, but really the sweet spot had started in Christ, and that's where it still is.

As we believe in our hearts and confess with our mouths that God raised Jesus from the dead, we are saved. Many people stop there, but we don't have to.

You can move from religion to relationship. You can come to Him wherever you are on your journey. You can find your sweet spot. It's not the end. There is more in store.

It's not too late. With God, all things are possible. Welcome to the sweet spot. Yes, I can. Yes, you can. God bless you.

ABOUT THE AUTHOR

Leslie V, founder of Finding Your Sweet Spot, is committed to helping people understand how to fulfill their God-given destiny and unlock hope, clarity, and confidence. Leslie has hosted online summits on this topic with over twenty-one influencers, as well as her own podcast, Motivation Meditation with Leslie V. Along with her mom, Mattie, Leslie is part of the Praise and Worship Team of her church, helping people hear the words that can help them move through life to find their sweet spot.

Leslie V had always loved the church she grew up in; it was an integral part of her life, her family, and her relationship with God. Then one day she heard something different, something that caught her attention. She heard the teaching of the Word of God, and she liked it. She wanted to know more about what God was bringing into her life. This desire would lead her on a journey, one filled with challenges, signs and messages, to the church that was truly right for her. It led her to find her sweet spot.

As you take the journey with her, you will understand that God made you for more than the life you are currently living. No matter the difficulties, you too can step out of your comfort zone, explore your gifts, and reach for the dreams He has placed in your heart. You too can find your sweet spot.